RESPECT FOR PERSONS

RESPECT FOR PERSONS

by

R. S. DOWNIE

Senior Lecturer in Moral Philosophy
at the University of Glasgow

and

ELIZABETH TELFER

Lecturer in Moral Philosophy
at the University of Glasgow

London
GEORGE ALLEN AND UNWIN LTD
RUSKIN HOUSE · MUSEUM STREET

PRINTED IN GREAT BRITAIN
in 11 pt Imprint 1 point leaded
BY C. TINLING AND CO LTD
LIVERPOOL, LONDON AND
PRESCOT

To
W.G.M.

PREFACE

THE idea of the individual person as of supreme worth is fundamental to the moral, political and religious ideals of our society. It
has correspondingly been given a central place in such basic
philosophical works as Kant's *Groundwork of the Metaphysic of
Morals* or J. S. Mill's *On Liberty*. There is a need, however, for a
sustained examination of the idea in the language of contemporary
analytical philosophy, and the aim of this essay is to satisfy such a
need.

Our strategy is to discuss in Chapter I the meanings of such
terms as 'respect' and 'end', whether a principle or an attitude is
mainly involved, and so on. In Chapter II we show that the
ordinary rules and judgements of social morality presuppose
respect for persons as their ultimate ground, while in Chapter III
we argue that there is also an area of private or self-referring
morality—that there is more to morality than its social dimension—
and that it too presupposes respect for persons as its ultimate
ground. The first three chapters, taken together, represent our
attempt to clarify the moral ideas characterized by 'respect for
persons as ends'. In Chapters IV and V—the second main
division of the book—we go on to consider what the morality of
respect for persons permits or requires by way of metaphysical and
meta-ethical positions. We argue in Chapter IV that it requires an
irreducibly purposive interpretation of action, and that it is the
possibility of this (non-determinist) interpretation of purposive
concepts which justifies our ascriptions of moral responsibility. In
Chapter V we begin by discussing the general logical features of
respect-for-persons morality—the most controversial of which is
that moral judgements have the logical status of expressions of
belief—and conclude that while a prescriptivist meta-ethics (the
'commitment theory') is inappropriate, respect-for-persons morality permits either a naturalistic meta-ethics (the 'good reasons
theory') or a non-naturalistic meta-ethics. The theory of non-
naturalism is rarely stated with any plausibility by analytic
philosophers, but we try to present it more sympathetically and to
show that it can in fact meet the arguments against it which are
commonly regarded as decisive.

Our hope is that the book may be of interest to students not only of moral and political philosophy but also of the philosophies of religion and education. For we provide an analysis of the Judaeo-Christian concept of *agape*, and in general present in secular or humanistic terms a view of morality which is characteristically expounded by Judaeo-Christian thinkers. And we discuss in detail concepts which are crucial to educational theory—such as self-realization, self-respect, 'worth-while activities' and 'respect for persons' itself.

We owe debts to many people, but in particular to three. Eileen Downie has helped us with both substance and style, and has acted as peace-maker in the fights which arose in this joint philosophical venture, and Professor D. D. Raphael has given us the experienced advice of one who knows the pitfalls in our kind of territory. Finally, Professor W. G. Maclagan has provided detailed criticism of every chapter and has encouraged us to develop our central theme. In gratitude for his assistance, and in recognition of the general philosophical inspiration he has provided for us and many other pupils and colleagues, we should like to dedicate this book to him on the occasion of his retirement.

University of Glasgow

CONTENTS

CHAPTER I

RESPECT FOR PERSONS
AS ENDS

1. ENDS

THERE is something odd about speaking of *persons* as ends, although this oddity does not strike one at first because the Kantian formula is so familiar. One begins to see it as odd, however, if one considers what is meant by an 'end'. The term is ambiguous, but it is used to mean, in the first place, a purpose, aim or objective. It is therefore something which can (logically) be desired and brought about. But can one speak of 'desiring and bringing about persons'? This does not seem to be intelligible (in any relevant sense), and the reason is that a category mistake is involved. To bring this out let us consider the category of that which can be desired or brought about.

The category of what can be desired or brought about seems to be that of a situation or state of affairs. It may be objected that we can speak of desiring a *thing* ('I want an apple') or *to do* something ('I want to sing and skip about'). But this difficulty is only apparent. For when a man wants a thing, he wants some state of affairs to come about which did not obtain before, viz his having or possessing the thing; or else he wants the present situation, viz his possessing the thing, to continue. And when a man wants to do something or wants someone else to do something, we can say that he wants a new state of affairs to begin in which this activity is taking place, or that he wants the present state of activity on his part or another's to continue. We can therefore characterize the category of the object of desire as a situation or state of affairs which is to be brought about or maintained; and when one talks of 'desiring an x' it is usually clear from the context and the sense of 'x' what state of affairs is in question in any given case. A *person* cannot therefore be an end in this sense because it is not clear how he is linked with a situation which can be desired or brought about.

It is true that his continued existence might be so described. But there is more to treating a person as an end than desiring his continued existence.

An 'end' can mean, in the second place, that which is desirable in itself. This sense of 'end' seems to be closer to what we are seeking, for it can be used to distinguish that which is desirable as a means from that which is desirable as an end; and this distinction seems to have connexions with treating people as means and treating them as ends. It is true that there can be chains of means and ends, so that what in one context is desirable as an end may in another be desirable only as a means to a further end. For example, the winning of the battle may be desirable as a means to the desirable end of winning the war; but the winning of the war can itself be viewed as a means to the further desirable end of a political settlement. Yet chains of means and ends must stop somewhere, and where they stop we have an end-in-itself. Can we say that persons are ends desirable in themselves?

We cannot, for once again we are in the wrong category: that which is desirable can necessarily be desired and, as we have argued, all that logically can be desired are situations or states of affairs; but persons are not situations or states of affairs. Thus, while the sense of 'end' which means 'that which is desirable' enables us to introduce the distinction, certainly relevant to our purposes, of means and ends, it does not enable us to identify the sense in which we can speak of persons as ends.

There is, however, a third sense in which 'end' can be used: an 'end' can mean 'that which is valuable in itself'. It may be thought that the distinction between the desirable and the valuable is merely one of linguistic style. But this is not so, for in discussing the valuable we are not restricted to situations or states of affairs; a thing or an activity can be said to be valuable in itself. Moreover, the distinction between means and ends is still relevant to this sense of 'end'; we can speak of something being valuable as a means or being valuable as an end. Now to regard something as being valuable merely as a means is to regard it as valuable merely for what one can get out of it—it is no more than useful. A valuable thing which is not merely a means is valuable in itself. It should be noted that to say that a thing is valuable in itself is not to exclude the possibility that it is valuable *also* as a means and can be regarded or treated as a means; it is to say only that it is not *merely* a means.

Applying this to persons, we can say that the meaning of the injunction to treat and regard people not merely as means but also as ends is that we ought to treat them as valuable in themselves and not only as useful instruments. Certainly, the postman is used to deliver our letters, but it is wrong to regard him solely under that description.

So far we have tried to show that respecting a person as an end means regarding him and treating him as something which is not merely useful but also valuable in itself. The task which remains is that of trying to explain what is meant by a thing's or a person's being valuable in itself in those cases which cannot be explained by equating this description with 'desirable in itself'.

Roughly, a situation which is desirable in itself is one which should be *brought about* because of what it is, while a thing which is valuable in itself is one which should be *cherished* because of what it is. The expression 'because of what it is' suggests not only why it is valuable but also what cherishing it amounts to; to cherish a thing is to care about its essential features—those which, as we say, 'make it what it is'—and to consider important not only that it should continue to exist but also that it should flourish. Hence, to respect a person as an end is to respect him for those features which make him what he is as a person and which, when developed, constitute his flourishing.

2. RULES, PRINCIPLES AND ATTITUDES

There is sometimes ambiguity, when 'respect for persons' is spoken of as a moral *principle*, as to whether it is *one* of our basic principles, on a par, say, with principles dealing with truth-telling or promise-keeping (if we assume for the moment that they are on a par with each other) or whether it is the basic moral principle. If the first interpretation is adopted, then to respect persons as ends will be one of the many specific requirements of the moral life; if the second, the principle will sum up or characterize what all the other specific requirements have in common—they will all be ways or modes of respecting persons. If we adopt the second interpretation we can regard the many specific requirements of morality as reflecting the existence of moral *rules*, while 'respect for persons as ends' will express their supreme regulative *principle*. The second interpretation is the one adopted and defended in this essay.

Now to regard 'respect for persons' as the supreme regulative principle of morality still leaves unresolved an ambiguity as to its category. For sometimes philosophers speak of it as a *principle*, but sometimes as an *attitude*. What is the relationship between a principle and an attitude?

The term 'attitude' is used a good deal in recent moral philosophy, but the frequency of its occurrence is probably connected with its convenient lack of precision. For example, Professor P. Nowell-Smith is explicit that he has chosen the term 'attitude' in his expressions 'pro-' and 'con-attitude' precisely because it is vague, and he is not even bothered by the fact that some of the items in his lists of pro- and con-attitudes are not really attitudes at all.[1] Professor R. M. Hare is more definite in the meaning he attaches to the term.[2] He writes that if the term 'attitude' means anything, it means a principle of action. But while it is certainly correct to say that an attitude will necessarily have connexions with principles of action, the connexion cannot be one of identity, for the notion of an attitude is wider than that of a principle of action. Thus, it may not be possible to tell from knowledge of the principle on which a man acted what his attitude was towards his action. For example, if we know that a man makes it a principle of action to have a cold bath in the mornings we still cannot tell from this knowledge alone even such basic things as whether his attitude towards cold baths is *pro* or *con*; he may like them, or he may dislike them but have a pro-attitude towards health or towards a reputation for endurance. What, then, is the connexion between an attitude and a principle of action?

There are two connexions, one logical and one causal. There is a logical connexion in that if a person has a certain attitude towards something he will necessarily adopt certain principles of action towards it *other things being equal*, and the general nature of the principles can be inferred from knowledge of the attitude. We need to add the qualification in order to allow for conflicting attitudes. Thus, if a man has an attitude of fear towards cows, he will (other things being equal) adopt a principle of avoiding cows; but if he has another attitude which is one of humiliation and self-loathing towards the first attitude, he may well make it a principle to walk through fields of cows as often as he can, hoping to cure himself. We can make this point in another way by saying that certain principles of action are logically connected with certain attitudes in so far as these attitudes can be regarded as working in isolation.

As can be seen in the example of the man's attitude towards cows, the connexion between an attitude and a principle can also be causal. For, even although a person does not have a certain attitude, if he consistently acts on a certain principle he may find he has acquired the attitude; to act *as if* one had a certain attitude may be the first step, and a necessary one, in acquiring the attitude.

If we apply this analysis to 'respect for persons as ends' we find that the expression can refer both to an attitude and to a principle of action. The attitude is *logically* basic in that the principle has to be explained in terms of it; it is the principle which logically must be adopted (other things being equal) by someone who has the attitude of respect. But it is also *morally* basic in that it includes in its scope modes of feeling and thinking as well as of acting; and that which is morally fundamental is a total quality of life rather than a principle of action in the narrow sense. Our primary task is therefore to attempt to characterize the attitude of respect for persons. This will be the main concern of the present chapter, and in the next two we shall go on to consider in more detail the principles or rules of action to which this attitude may give rise. It should also be noted that the causal connexion between the principle of action and the attitude is important, for it will enable us at a later stage to meet the objection that sometimes a person may not be able to act with a certain attitude: he can always act on a principle and thus take the first step towards acquiring or revitalizing the attitude. In the meantime, as a necessary preliminary to investigating the attitude of respect, let us consider further what it is to have an attitude.

3. ATTITUDES

The most important point about an attitude (for our purposes) may be brought out if we say that an attitude is two-sided. In the first place, it must be an attitude *of* something, where 'something' is always a disposition of some sort, such as hope, fear, distrust, forbearance or the like. In the second place, attitudes must be *to* something; it is conceptually impossible for an attitude to lack an object. It will be possible to describe this object in various ways, but for any particular attitude there will be one description under which the object of the attitude must by definition fall. For example, an attitude cannot logically be one of hope unless it is to an object which is believed to be in some sense a good to the hoper. The connexion between hope and an imagined good is thus a necessary one, and we might go as far as to say that a person could not understand the meaning of 'hope' unless he knew what it was to imagine a good, and that to imagine a good is to lay the foundation for acquiring the concept of hope. A similar analysis applies to all attitudes; they can be identified by means of the characteristics which their object is believed to possess, and thus a belief is at the root of all attitudes. The object under the description which is implied by the attitude-name may be called the *formal object* of that attitude. For example, the formal object of hope is an imagined good, which, it is believed, may come about, and the formal object of fear is a believed danger, and so on. Of course, this specification of the formal object of an attitude leaves quite open the answers to two further totally separate questions: what can (empirically) fall under a formal-object description—in the case of fear, for example, what can in fact be regarded by human beings as dangerous; and what should fall under it—what can truly or appropriately be regarded as dangerous. The first of these questions will be empirical; the second will be partly empirical but also partly evaluative, since the answer to it will depend in the last resort on our view of good and evil. They are thus quite different from any question as to the nature of the formal object of an attitude, which is really a conceptual question about the attitude itself.

What is the formal object of the attitude of respect? Of the several relevant senses of 'to respect' the one basic to 'respect for persons' was that of 'to value' or 'to esteem'; to respect persons is to value them as persons. It seems, then, that the formal object of the attitude we are investigating is something like 'that which is thought valuable or estimable'; respecting something implies thinking it valuable or estimable. Thus, to understand in more detail what it means to respect persons we must find out why persons are regarded as valuable. Why, then, do we respect or value persons?

4. PERSONS

It may be said that we value people because of their merits; and merits vary a good deal. For example, we may respect, in the sense of 'value', one man for his courage while we may value another for his integrity. Now, if it is the case that we value people because of their merits, then, since people's merits vary, there seems to be a problem about understanding what it is about persons as such that we value; for it does not seem easy to compile a list of merits characterizing people as such in virtue of which they are objects of esteem or respect. A possible answer to the problem is to be found if we try to compile a list of those features which constitute the 'generic' human 'self' or are the 'distinctive endowment of a human being' (to use Mill's phrase).[3] Now the items on such a list would not exactly be merits in the sense in which integrity, say, is a merit; but they might nevertheless be the qualities which human beings value in themselves, for they would make up the 'distinctive endowment of a human being'. Moreover, there is a connexion between valuing the 'distinctive endowment' of a human being (his 'generic' self) and valuing his specific merits or individuality (his 'idiosyncratic' self); for the development of the distinctive endowment will, granted the existence of idiosyncratic variations in human beings, lead to the production of specific merits. Let us at any rate assume the validity of this approach and enquire what is the distinctive endowment of a human being, or what constitutes the 'generic' human self.

Before we try to answer this question, however, we should become clear about what kind of question it is. It is not merely an investigation into what distinguishes humans from other animals. This can be seen by considering whether we would call such things as differences in the number and type of teeth, or in the way hair is distributed on the body, part of the 'distinctive endowment' of a human being. Rather we are looking for the most important difference between humans and other animals, where 'important' indicates an *evaluative judgement* which picks out certain features rather than others (as the evaluative word 'endowment' suggests). It may seem that we are simply *analysing* the concept of a person in an evaluatively neutral manner. But the concept of a *person* is already an evaluative concept with something of the force of 'that which makes a human being valuable' implied in it, and this is even more true of the more abstract concept 'personality'. Thus, our original question, 'Why do we respect or value persons?' can be put in another way: 'What makes a human being a *person* (with all that that implies)?'

An objection may be raised here to the emphasis we have placed on the evaluative nature of the concept of a person: namely, that it makes the dictum 'Persons ought to be respected' trivial, if not indeed analytic. But this would be a mistaken objection. The concept of a person retains a connexion with the less evaluative concept of a human being. Thus, to say 'Persons ought to be respected' is not merely to say 'What is valuable ought to be respected', but rather, 'Humans ought to be respected for what is valuable in them'. And this is not a trivial claim, for it asserts that there is something worthy of respect about a human being. We can now return to our enquiry into the distinctive nature of a human being, having tried to clarify the nature of this enquiry.

Traditionally it has been assumed that basic to the distinctive endowment of a human being is his ability to reason, and it may be helpful to discuss this view in terms of the Kantian thesis that what gives a person absolute worth is his possession of a rational will. An initial objection to this claim might be that there is surely more to human nature than an ability to reason. Such an objection would misconceive what is meant by a 'rational will', for to have a rational will is to be capable not simply of thinking rationally but also of acting rationally; to accept the concept of 'rational will' is to commit oneself to the view that reason can be practical as well as theoretical. What is involved in the practical exercise of reason?

It involves, in the first place, the ability to choose for oneself, and, more extensively, to formulate purposes, plans and policies of one's own. A second and closely connected element is the ability to carry out decisions, plans or policies without undue reliance on the help of others. These two abilities are connected by a kind of pragmatic necessity, in that the ability to decide requires for its development the concurrent development of the ability to execute. The importance we attach to these manifestations of the rational will is reflected in our firm approval of such traits of character as 'being able to stand on one's own feet', 'being relatively independent of others', 'sticking to one's guns', 'knowing what one wants, or what one ought to do', 'having aims in one's life (as distinct from being aimless)', 'knowing one's own mind' and 'being able to decide for oneself'. The necessary connexion between developing such traits of character and being a person is reflected in theories of education which stress the importance of cultivating such dispositions in children. Conversely, to impair a person's abilities to formulate and carry out aims and policies of his own devising is to that extent to destroy him as a person. For example, if a person is injured physically or mentally there is often a tendency for friends to help too much; it is often easier to do something for people than to wait patiently and encourage while they do it for themselves, and this ease and convenience can assume the guise of kindness. But this may well be a subtle way of eroding an individual's nature as a person. The development of personality can also be blocked on a grander scale by political arrangements which restrict the range of images which people can form of themselves, as (perhaps) in Communist China. The exercise of the rational will involved in the foregoing examples are expressions of the first feature which makes up the distinctive endowment of a human being. Let us call it the ability to be self-determining. It is clearly important in any analysis of what is valuable in human personality. But there is a second feature—much stressed by Kant—involved in the possession of a rational will: the ability to govern one's conduct by rules, and indeed, more grandly, to adopt rules which one holds to be binding on oneself and all rational beings. This feature of the exercise of rational will is the one which most clearly distinguishes man from animals, for whereas some animals may possess to a slight extent the ability to carry out plans of their own devising (Köhler's apes)—or at least to act in ways which invite the use of such language—it is not plausible to suggest that they can have a conception of a rule, far less adopt rules for themselves. The ability to shape one's conduct in terms of rules, and to adopt (or even create) rules valid for all men, is called by Kant the autonomy of the will, and in the autonomy of the will Kant sees the very essence of personality. In Chapter V we shall cast doubt on one aspect of this Kantian conception—the notion of self-validating moral legislation—but meanwhile we can take from Kant the weaker thesis that human beings are not only self-determining but also formulate and follow rules, some of which (such as moral rules) they hold to be binding on others besides themselves.

It might be objected that the analysis has not yet mentioned emotions, feelings or desires. Yet they surely contribute something of distinctive value to human personality. Now it would be unfair to Kant to say that he saw no value at all in sentience, but he certainly did not see it as contributing anything to the intrinsic worth of a person; this he restricted to the exercise of reason in a narrower sense. But it may be that the sharp distinction between reason and sentience accepted by Kant and other philosophers is artificial. Sentience in the form in which it is characteristic of a person does involve reason. It is true that some animals may be able to experience certain emotions, but the ability to feel and express a wide range of sustained emotions is characteristically human, and it involves the perception and discrimination which only reason can supply. Hence, to see the value of the human person as lying in the ability to experience emotion is not to see anything which is inconsistent with the exercise of rational will; for in so far as emotions are characteristically human they necessarily involve rational will. In a similar way, the experience of complex desires involves rational will. The exercise of rational will is to be seen, then, as something at once (in old-fashioned terminology) cognitive, conative and affective, and it is the ability to exercise such a will in self-determination and rule-following which gives human personality its intrinsic value.

It should be noted that Kant sees the rational will as being necessarily free. Now it is certainly the case that if the concept is being used to indicate that a person is a centre of purposive activity in terms of rules, the rational will must be free in some sense. But whether it must be free in Kant's sense is a question which may be postponed till Chapter IV. Let us rather consider what objections may be made against the view that the value of the human person is to be seen in his distinctive endowment—the possession of a rational will.

The main objection to putting the concept of rational will at the centre of our analysis of human personality is that it seems to beg a number of questions about the nature of human action and purposiveness. We have been interpreting the characteristic endowment of a human being in terms of factors such as the ability to pursue ends, to create and adopt rules, to cultivate and sustain complex emotions. Now it may be said that to regard all these factors as necessarily involving or expressing rational will is to beg questions about the respective places of reason, feeling and desire in human life by giving the pride of place to reason without providing arguments to support this. There is a good deal of force in this objection, but, in mitigation, two points at least may be made. The first is that, as we have already stressed, to see the activity of reason in all these factors is by no means to imply that reason is the only thing operative in determining their nature; it is to stress only that without the activity of reason they could not have the nature they do in fact have. The second point is that some of the gaps in the detailed argument required to establish the practical force of reason will be supplied later in the discussion.* We shall therefore assume for the present that what is of value in persons can be characterized roughly as the exercise of rational will, taking that concept in a broad sense which does not exclude the concomitant presence of feeling and desire.[4]

5. RESPECTING PERSONS

It is now possible to make an attempt to explicate the concept of respect as it occurs in 'respect for persons'. We argued that the expression 'respect for persons' is used to indicate both an attitude which is commonly thought to be morally fundamental and a principle of action to be explained in terms of the attitude. The task of spelling out in detail the modes of conduct and of social organization which follow from the principle is reserved for the next two chapters and we shall be concerned here with analysing the nature of the attitude conveyed by the concept of respect. We can see what this attitude involves in the light of our account of the evaluative concept of a *person* (the concept which picks out those features of human nature which make it worthy of respect); this account was in terms of rational will. In the exercise of rational will there are two main features, which we have called 'self-determination' and 'rule-following', and allowance must be made for the different nature of each in our shaping of the concept of respect. Let us first consider self-determination.

Kant provides an example in the *Groundwork* which hints at what is required as a morally fitting attitude towards self-determination. He takes the case of a man for whom things are going well but who sees others, whom he could help, struggling with hardships. Kant supposes that this man says to himself, 'What does it matter to me? Let everyone be as happy as Heaven wills or as he can make himself; I won't deprive him of anything; I won't even envy him; only I have no wish to contribute anything to his well-being or to his support in distress'.[5] Now Kant holds that such an attitude is not the worst possible, but he also holds that a will which decided to act in such a manner 'would be in conflict with itself, since many a

* See Chapter V.

situation might arise in which the man needed love and sympathy from others, and in which . . . he would rob himself of all hope of the help he wants'. The point emerges more clearly when Kant discusses the same example again in another context.[6] He writes that 'the natural end which all men seek is their own happiness. Now humanity could no doubt subsist if everybody contributed nothing to the happiness of others but at the same time refrained from deliberately impairing their happiness. This is, however, merely to agree negatively and not positively with humanity as an end in itself unless everyone endeavours also, so far as in him lies, to further the ends of others. For the ends of a subject who is an end in himself must, if this conception is to have its *full* effect in me, be also, as far as possible, *my* ends.' Kant is here suggesting that we should treat the ends of others, their ends of inclination, or what they pursue in the exercise of their self-determination, as if they were our own.

Now if respecting persons as self-determining agents involves positive concern for them of this nature it will involve what is best characterized by the concept of sympathy. But 'sympathy' can mean various things, and we shall have to qualify it to distinguish the relevant sense.

Professor W. G. Maclagan distinguishes three meanings of 'sympathy' (while admitting that other meanings may be possible).[7] The first he calls 'animal sympathy', by which he means a sort of 'psychological infection of one creature by another, as when panic fear spreads in a herd', and even in a human context there is 'in the operation of such animal sympathy, little or no sense of others as independent individual centres of experience. What we have is rather a sense of an indeterminate psychological atmosphere . . .'. In the second place, there is what Maclagan terms 'passive sympathy' or 'empathy'. This is sympathy in a distinctively human mode because, while there may be no clear line between it and animal sympathy, passive sympathy does involve consciousness of others as experiencing subjects. It is a matter of 'feeling oneself into the experience of the other' or of an emotional 'identification of ourself with the other'. The third form of sympathy, which Maclagan distinguishes as 'active sympathy', is the 'sympathy of practical *concern for* others as distinguished from simply *feeling with* them'. Now sympathy in the third of Maclagan's senses is the concept we require to analyse the example which Kant provided of a man who did not help others in pursuing their ends of inclination. Such a man did not show respect for persons as ends, and he did not do so because his conduct lacked the concern for others expressed in the concept of 'active sympathy'. We must therefore make room for this concept in our account of what it is to respect persons as rational wills.

It should be noted by way of qualification that in showing active sympathy for people—in making their ends our own—we must be careful not to help too much, as we argued in discussing the concept of self-determination. It is possible to secure a man's ends for him at the price of impairing his ability to pursue ends for himself, and so a morally fitting attitude towards self-determination must temper the giving of assistance to others with due regard for their ability to execute their own purposes.

Now at this point an objection may be lodged against our claim that active sympathy is a necessary ingredient in the concept of respect as we are using it. For we are proposing 'respect for persons' as a characterization of the ideal moral attitude, but it may be said that all the components in a moral attitude must be under the control of the will. What has been called 'active sympathy', however, seems to be a gift of nature—some may have it, others not—and it is a mistake to make a gift of nature a necessary ingredient in a moral attitude, especially the supreme one. Indeed, the argument may go on, Kant himself in an earlier passage seems to admit the possibility that a man may have by nature little or no sympathy with the sufferings of others, but he stresses that such a man, however cold or indifferent by temperament, could none the less help others not from inclination but from a sense of duty. (And he seems to have an admiration for such a person.) The objection, then, is that we cannot make sympathy a necessary ingredient of the supreme attitude of morality (however it may add grace to the moral life) because not everyone has been given a sympathetic nature. Moreover, we can do without it, for, if we are to believe Kant, it is possible to do one's duty without sympathy.

In replying to the objection we may first of all deny that it is in fact possible to do all that is implied in the attitude of respect for persons without active sympathy. It may be possible to go through the outward motions of actions which conform to duty without such sympathy, but the creative and imaginative exercise of the moral life is not possible without active sympathy. What, then, are we to say of the point that sympathy is a gift unevenly distributed by nature, and as such is unsuitable as an ingredient in a *moral* attitude? The answer is to insist that the relevant form of sympathy is not so unevenly distributed that it cannot form the basis of the supreme attitude of morality. And here again we may borrow an argument from Maclagan.[8]

Maclagan argues that what he has called 'passive sympathy' or 'empathy' is a natural capacity, 'natural not only as contrasted with moral but also as opposed to unnatural'. It may be inhibited in some cases, like other natural capacities, and what inhibits the growth of passive sympathy is an extreme of self-concern. 'If and so far as we can escape from obsession with ourselves, passive empathetic sympathy, I suggest, flowers in our experience quite naturally.' Now it may be argued that, even if we concede that passive human sympathy is a capacity in every normal human make-up, we have not shown that this is true of active sympathy, and it is active sympathy which is required if we are to see in the attitude of respect a practical concern for other persons as such. The answer suggested by Maclagan is that it is psychologically impossible to sympathize with someone in the passive mode without at the same time having some measure of active concern for him. In fact, Maclagan goes as far as to doubt whether there are even *pathological* instances to the contrary in this matter.

We might indeed wonder whether there is not a *conceptual* connexion between active and passive sympathy. For if passive sympathy involves sharing to some extent the feelings of others, must this not also mean sharing to some extent in the actions which are the expression of those feelings? If someone has a certain aim and we share with him his feelings about this aim, then, just as the existence of his own feelings implies the existence of a motivation to appropriate action, so we too will be motivated to take steps to fulfil the aim (to make his ends our own). In fact, the difficulty may be to prevent the identification of our feelings and his, and therefore of our policies, from becoming too complete; we may need to remind ourselves that the other man's aim is often not merely that he should in the end have something, but also that he should acquire it by his own efforts. The argument, then, is that active sympathy is necessarily connected with passive sympathy, and passive sympathy is a capacity which is the possession of all normal beings. It is therefore permissible to make active sympathy an ingredient in the attitude of respect, when that attitude is directed towards persons conceived as exercising self-determination in the pursuit of objects of inclination.

Support for the view that a natural capacity, such as that for sympathetic feeling, can be a permissible element in a moral attitude is to be obtained from a paper by Professor Bernard Williams.[9] Williams points out that the emotions are passively experienced, but he does not regard this fact as counting against their moral importance. On the contrary, he argues that the element of passivity 'may itself make a vital contribution to the notion of moral sincerity'. There are, of course, as Williams admits, important distinctions to be drawn between various kinds of natural capacity—some will be more relevant to a moral attitude than others—but 'among the relevant sorts of characteristic, the capacity for creative emotional response has the advantage of being, if not equally, at least broadly, distributed'. Our claim is that active sympathy is one form of 'creative emotional response', and that it is a response to the conception of persons as self-determining agents pursuing ends of inclination. As such it is a necessary component in the attitude of respect.

It may be added here that those who object to our making the natural capacity for sympathy an ingredient in the moral attitude of respect may have failed to grasp the distinction between an attitude and a principle. We said at the beginning of the chapter that acting on a principle was causally connected with the possession of an attitude, in that a man can always act on a principle and hence develop in himself the connected attitude. In the light of the present discussion we can supplement this by saying that if a man possesses the raw material of an attitude, in the form of some measure of the appropriate feelings, he can develop it by acting appropriately; and whereas the strength of an attitude may not always be under the direct control of a man's will, it is always possible for him to adopt the principle of action which will develop the germs of active sympathy which (we hold) everyone possesses, and thus strengthen his moral attitude.

It was argued that people are not only self-determining but also rule-following. This feature of persons also moulds the attitude of respect. The nature of the modification it requires in the attitude of respect may be seen if we draw a specific distinction which brings out one of the most important aspects of rule-following. The distinction is between forgiving and condoning.[10] Let us suppose that A has been injured by B. A may condone the injury in the sense of treating it lightly. Now there may be contexts in which this attitude of condonation is morally appropriate—especially where the injury is trivial—but it may not always be morally appropriate. To play down an injury may be morally inappropriate in that it represents an attempt to minimize the fact that rules which both parties accept have been violated. In other words, an attitude of condonation may be an inappropriate one to adopt towards a person in that it ignores the fact that he is able to satisfy rules as well as pursue certain purposes. To condone is to fail to respect persons in that it is to ignore one of the features essential to being a person—the ability to adopt and satisfy rules.

But a second point emerges from the distinction between forgiving and condoning. For B may reject A's rules, and so deny the need for forgiveness. Now sometimes of course B's position may be justified. But in establishing this B ought to take into account the possibility that A's rules apply to him also. This is the point which Kant expresses in terms of his often-parodied thesis of universal legislation. Kant assumes that all men, in so far as they are rational, will legislate in the same way. Such a conception can be only an ideal, but the truth it exaggerates is that in dealing with others we ought to reveal in our attitudes a realization that the rules in terms of which they act may also be valid for us. In so far as we are in moral disagreement with other persons our attitude towards them ought to display a realization that we could be mistaken, and that their rules could be the valid ones.

The same point can be made in terms of reasons. For in seeing persons as essentially rule-following we are conceiving of them as rational agents who are able to act or forbear because they can see good reasons for their actions. We ought therefore to consider how far their reasoning may apply to us.

Let us now try to tie together the various components in our attitude of respect. In so far as persons are thought of as self-determining agents who pursue objects of interest to themselves we respect them by showing active sympathy with them; in Kant's language, we make their ends our own. In so far as persons are thought of as rule-following we respect them by taking seriously the fact that the rules by which they guide their conduct constitute reasons which may apply both to them and to ourselves. In the attitude of respect we have, then, two necessary components: an attitude of active sympathy and a readiness at least to consider the applicability of other men's rules both to them and to ourselves. These two components are independently necessary and jointly sufficient to constitute the attitude of respect which it is fitting to direct at persons, conceived as rational wills.

It is arguable that an attitude so constituted may best be described as one of love. Now many different kinds of attitude may be called 'love', but the relevant kind seems to be what in the language of the Gospels is called *agape*. The term *agape* is not without its own obscurities but it seems the most suitable for characterizing an attitude which combines a regard for others as rule-following with an active sympathy with them in their pursuit of ends. It is an attitude illustrated in the story of the Good Samaritan, and again in the well-known passage from St John's Gospel: 'Greater love hath no man than this, that a man lay down his life for his friends'. To lay down one's life for one's friends may be a supreme example of making the ends of others one's own, but it should also be noted that to *accept* such sacrifice may also be to show respect or *agape* because such acceptance may be an expression of the recognition that others too are moral agents who can follow rules and display the attitude of *agape* in their lives.

We argued earlier that attitudes necessarily have formal objects, and that understanding what is meant by the name of an attitude involves knowing what its formal object is. We said that the formal object of respect is 'that which is thought valuable', and that those aspects of human beings in virtue of which they fall under this description—those aspects which are thought valuable—are summed up by the expressions 'a person' and 'personality'. Our ability to arrive at some notion of what constitutes personality was thus dependent on a prior idea, however vague, of what 'respect' means. Having arrived at this notion of personality, we were then able to show more precisely what is involved in valuing and esteeming personality, and have in effect tailored the attitude to fit its object, trimming off what does not apply to an attitude directed towards persons as we have defined them. This attitude we have called *agape*, and since it has been defined to fit the concept of a person, it can be said that 'a person' is the formal object of *agape*. Thus, just as 'Hope is always for an imagined good' is an analytic judgement, so '*Agape* is always felt towards those regarded as persons' is an analytic judgement. But, as we shall see in the next section, this fact leaves open the possibility of debate as to who or what is properly or truly to be regarded as a person, as there can be debate about whether something hoped for is really good or not.

Now a difficulty arises if we regard persons as the formal object of *agape*. The difficulty can best be seen if we consider first the analogy we have already used—that of hope and its formal object, viz something which may come about and which is thought to be good. It seems to be the case that if something which may come about is *in fact* good then it logically follows that it ought to be hoped for. In the same way, if something is in fact dangerous it logically follows that it ought to be feared. This logical feature of the relationship between hope or fear and their formal objects does not hold of all verbs and their formal objects. For example, the formal object of 'divorce' is 'a spouse', but it does not follow from this that if someone really is my spouse I ought to divorce him or her. What distinguishes hope and fear is that they and their formal objects are *evaluative*, and in this they resemble *agape* and its formal object, a person. But if *agape* is like hope and fear in this way, it may be argued that 'Persons ought to be respected' becomes analytic, in the same way that 'The dangerous ought to be feared' is analytic. If this were so, the respect-for-persons principle could no longer be regarded as a basic moral principle, because it would be empty of content.

This difficulty can however be met if we recall the argument of Section 5. As we saw there, the notion of a person has a good deal of descriptive content—far more than the notions of the good or the dangerous. It retains its connexion with the non-evaluative concept of a human being, even though it may be appropriate to extend the notion of 'person' to include the non-human also. Because of the high descriptive content of the notion of a person, we can say 'Persons ought to be respected' without triviality. For to say 'Persons ought to be respected' or 'Persons ought to be regarded with *agape*' is to say not merely 'What is valuable ought to be respected' but rather 'Human beings (and other creatures like them in the relevant respects) ought to be respected for what is valuable in them'.

6. OBJECTIONS

A number of objections may be raised to this account of what it is to respect persons. A radical objection may be that there is something unrealistic about the whole idea of respecting persons, for a 'person' is an abstraction; we in fact encounter *personae* or persons in various social roles. Now the truth in this objection is that the idea of the pure individual isolated from social influence is an abstraction. Indeed, it is not just that we are in some external way moulded by the social roles we adopt, but rather that our very identity as persons is constituted by the relationships in which we are placed by our social roles. Consider, for example, not only the occupational roles of lawyer, teacher or postman but also roles which enter into the depths of personal life such as those of husband, daughter or friend. It is therefore true to say that there is no such thing as the pure ego uncontaminated by social influences; and to that extent the idea of a 'role' as a *mere* part one can play while remaining essentially unaffected by it is misleading. But it does not follow from this that the idea of 'respect for persons' is an abstraction.

In the first place, it may be doubted whether all that we do is done in a role. There are many simple, spontaneous acts of kindness, malice or high spirits which do not proceed from one's conception of a role. A much more important point, however, is that even when we act in roles it is as *persons* that we are acting. 'Role' is a concept of social description and it is a useful tool for grouping duties, revealing structure in apparently unconnected activities and identifying various forms of social pressure. But this must not lead us to ignore the fact that it is *people* who perform the duties, pursue the activities and experience the pressures. If the idea of a pure ego is an abstraction, so is that of a role which is enacted without leaving the imprint of the person who is in the role. Hence, even if it is conceded that we never meet a person who is not in a role, this in no way suggests that it is not really a person whom we meet. Indeed, a common moral failing is to attend too much to a person's social role and not enough to the fact of his personality; to have contempt for him because he is a dustman or over-deference towards him because he is a television actor. Along these lines lies the sort of 'respect for persons' which is a vice, corrected, or over-corrected, by being 'no respecter of persons'.

The objections to regarding a person as simply a set of roles are developed by Professor Bernard Williams in his analysis of what it is to respect a person.[11] Williams points out that, in the first place, there is a distinction 'between regarding a man's life and character from an aesthetic or technical point of view, and regarding them from a point of view which is concerned primarily with what it is *for him* to live that life and do those actions in that character. . . . The technical or professional attitude is that which regards the man solely under that title as "miner" or "agricultural labourer" or "junior executive", the human approach that which regards him as *a man who has* that title (among others) willingly, unwillingly. . . .' As a development of this distinction, Williams argues, in the second place, that involved in the notion of treating each man as an end is the point that 'each man is owed an effort of identification: that he should not be regarded as the surface to which a certain label can be applied, but one should try to see the world (including the label) from his point of view'. Now a man can be so exploited that he will be unable to see himself as other than one who has a certain role, and this leads Williams to make the third point that respecting a person involves the avoidance of any policy that will suppress or destroy a man's consciousness of himself as one who has purposes and policies other than those given him by a certain role. And one might add here (extending Williams' argument) that a man can *himself* inhibit or even destroy his own consciousness of himself as a *person* who happens to occupy a given role and who may have purposes other than those of the role: the student who plays all the time at being a student, the over-officious civil servant and the too-charming salesman are examples of this. The phenomenon has indeed been explored by Sartre in his literary and philosophical writings. The three points made by Williams (with this extension) help to clarify the claim that, however much a person may be moulded by his social roles, we feel that he ought not to be regarded, or to regard himself, wholly in terms of the roles he occupies.

It might be objected that the concept of a person is itself a role-concept. In a discussion of this claim Professor Dorothy Emmet draws attention to the history which lies behind it.[12] She points out that one strand in Greek ethics sees the significance of a doctor as lying in his function (*ergon*) of being a doctor, and his 'virtue' in being a good doctor. This notion is extended by Aristotle and others to apply to a man as such, and we find bequeathed to the later Natural Law theorists the idea that 'human beings are not just members of the biological species *homo sapiens,* but can be seen as having a *social role* in the universe. So "natural" and "human" become role concepts with a normative overtone, calling attention to the obligation to live according to this social role.' There is a good deal of substance in this point. Certainly, as Professor Emmet points out, the concept of a social role is (perhaps unhelpfully) extended when one begins speaking of the role of a person as such. But this terminological point should not obscure the fact that the concept of a person is evaluative and has built into it conceptions, however undefined, of what a human being ought to be like. Still, to stress that the concept of person is thus evaluative is not to admit that personality can be analysed in terms of the *specific* roles in which a person may find himself in his daily life.

A central contention of the chapter has been that the attitude of respect for persons is *morally basic.* But a query may be raised as to whether, and if so, in what sense, this is the case; for the term 'basic' is ambiguous. It may mean that the attitude is paramount in the sense that in any conflict between it or a principle derived from it, and another attitude or principle, priority ought always to go to whatever policy seems to be required by *agape.* To interpret 'morally basic' in this way would allow for the possibility that some moral principles and attitudes have a basis other than that of the attitude of respect for persons. We wish to assert, however, that the attitude of respect for persons is morally basic in a stronger sense—that not only is it the paramount moral attitude but also that all other moral principles and attitudes are to be explained in terms of it. It is not easy to be sure that we can meet all the objections which may be raised to this thesis, but let us consider some of the more obvious ones.

In the first place, how is our admitted duty to seek the truth to be explained in terms of the attitude of respect for persons as ends? It should be noted that this question is not the same as the question how the duty to *tell* a person the truth is to be explained. The latter question can be answered by the reminder that to respect a person is to take into account in one's dealings with him that he is a rational creature able to shape his life in accordance with reasons, and that to tell him lies is to fail to take such factors into account. The former question concerns our duty to seek the truth or to seek

c

knowledge (and a similar difficulty can be raised over the duty to pursue art). The answer to this question cannot be fully developed until Chapter III, but it can be outlined at this stage. It is natural to assume that 'respect for persons' means respect for *other* persons, the attitude being interpreted as a social attitude and the principle as one of social morality. But, as we shall show, the attitude is also one of respect for humanity in one's own person—so much was stressed by Kant. Now we have argued that essential to being a person is the possession of a rational will; but such a feature, by its very nature, will lead a person to seek the truth. Hence, the duty to seek the truth is in fact derivative from the duty to act as a person.

But even if we grant that the duties to seek the truth and tell it can be explained in terms of respect for the humanity in one's own person, we are still left with some cases which are difficult to explain in terms of respect for persons. (And that they present difficulties to any theory of morality is not really an excuse for failing to make an attempt to account for them.) These are the cases of children, the senile, lunatics and animals. They present difficulties, for, while we do not regard it as a matter of moral indifference how we treat children, the senile, lunatics and animals, it is not clear that the attitude of respect for *persons* is appropriate because personality seems to be lacking, to a greater or lesser extent, in these cases. If respect and persons-as-rational-will are necessarily related, as we have been maintaining, can it be fitting to show *agape* towards the cases mentioned, and, if not, how can we account for our duties towards them?

The first step in meeting this difficulty is to point out that the relationship between *agape* and persons gives us the central cases of the concepts of *agape* and of persons—we would not properly know what *agape* meant unless we knew what it was to direct the attitude towards a person in the full sense—but that once we have the concept of *agape* it becomes possible to extend it to objects which are not persons in the full sense. Thus, children are potentially persons, and to some extent already persons although still children; and the senile are lapsed persons, although they may remain persons to some extent. It may be objected here that children and the senile are obviously persons in the full sense, and that speaking of them as 'potential persons' or 'lapsed persons' is misconceived. But this objection misses the point of our analysis of 'person'. Certainly, children and the senile are human beings in the full sense, but the word 'person' in our usage is a more precise term, implying the possession of capacities (to be self-determining and rule-following) which are not fully developed in children and may have decayed in the senile. It may further be objected, however, that congenital idiots have never been and will never be persons in the full sense. The answer is that there are still sufficient resemblances between them and persons to justify extending the language of *agape* to them, although it would not be possible to adopt such an attitude to them unless we first knew what it was to adopt it towards normal persons.

The second step in meeting the difficulty is to stress that there are other possible attitudes which are helpful in dealing with persons in this minimal sense. Affection, for instance, is perhaps the dominant attitude in a normal family atmosphere and as such it is what motivates parents and others in their dealings with children. Pity, again, is a powerful motive force which can lead people to care for the senile or congenital idiots, and if it is objected that not everyone can experience pity to a sufficient degree to lead them to care for the senile or congenital idiots, the answer is that not everyone *is* suitable for that job. Affection, pity and the like are not themselves moral attitudes, but they are consistent with *agape* and can reinforce it, while it in turn controls them when their natural springs are running dry, or are flowing too freely or becoming poisoned.

Can similar arguments be used to account for our moral duties to animals? There are, of course, views to the effect that we have no moral duties at all to animals as such; it is wrong to ill-treat animals only in so far as this is bad for the character of the ill-treater. (What lies behind this view is the claim that persons are to be respected in virtue of their possession of a soul, and since animals lack a soul they themselves can have no real claim on our respect.) But most people hold that we do have duties towards animals—or at least that we have the duty to avoid causing them unnecessary suffering. If then we are to succeed in explaining how all other moral principles and attitudes can be explained in terms of respect for persons, we shall need to show that animals have personality in some minimal sense. This can be done by suggesting that our duty to avoid causing them unnecessary suffering arises out of a respect for animals as, to a greater or lesser extent, *sentient* beings; and possession of sentience is not only a feature common to animals and human beings, but also the basis in the human being of the defining characteristics of personality—self-determination and the ability to follow rules.

In answering the foregoing objections we spoke of a person in the *full* sense as being the proper object of the attitude of *agape*, and argued that, once understood, such an attitude can be directed towards those who are not persons in this strict sense. But it may be objected to this that if we apply the word 'person' only to human beings we do not here have personality in the fullest sense. It may be said that to understand the nature of personality in the fullest sense we must consider the nature of God, and that hence God is the only proper object of respect or *agape*. We can therefore view human beings with respect only because they are made in the image of God.

Now if we consider the objection as a matter of the psychology of acquiring attitudes it cannot stand; we must first learn what it is to respect a person in the give-and-take of real life situations before we can direct the same attitude to an object we have not seen. So much indeed is no more than Scriptural.[13] It may be replied here that once we have acquired a grasp of the concepts of *agape* and of 'person' in a human context we require to apply them to the relationship between God and man to deepen our understanding of their proper meaning. But it is possible to deepen our understanding of *agape* and of personality by *imagining* a being called God who has the attributes and the attitude in a developed form, without presupposing the real existence of such a being. Hence, as a psychological thesis the objection is not damaging to our position.

The objection may be restated, however, in the form of a theological or philosophical thesis—that it is only so far as God loves us that we become proper objects of love for each other, or, in different words, that our value as human persons derives from the love which God has for us. Now this form of the objection, unlike the previous one, does require us to presuppose the existence of God. But let us, for the sake of argument, presuppose the non-existence of God. We are surely not forced to conclude (although some theologians have concluded) that personality thereby loses its value. And if we can see human personality as having value without presupposing the existence of God, *a fortiori* we are not obliged to see the value of personality as dependent on the prior love of God.

7. CONCLUSION

At this point we can tie together the conclusions so far reached. Basically, 'respect for persons as ends' refers to an attitude—a way of *regarding* persons—although the attitude will necessarily give rise to certain characteristic principles of action—ways of *treating* persons. To respect a person as an end is to value or cherish him for what he is—and that is a possessor of a rational will, where 'rational will' refers to the abilities to be self-determining and rule-following with all that these imply. To *respect* such a person is to make his ends one's own (show sympathy with him) and to take into account in all one's dealings with him that he too is self-determining and rule-following. In a word, to respect a person (so understood) is to have an attitude of *agape* towards him; and we can say that a person as a rational will is the formal object of the attitude of *agape*. To assert this is not to deny the influence of special roles and other social influences in moulding personality and giving content to duties. Such an attitude is morally basic not only in that it is paramount but also in that all other moral attitudes and principles can be explained in terms of it. This is not to exclude from moral attitudes creatures which have personality only in a minimal sense, for once we understand what it is to have respect for a person in the full sense (and a belief in God, while not essential to this understanding, may well aid it) we can then extend the attitude in a suitably modified form to whatever is thought to have traces of personality.

CHAPTER II

RESPECT FOR PERSONS
AND PUBLIC MORALITY

I. PUBLIC MORALITY

IN our first chapter we tried to elucidate in general terms the view that respect for persons as ends expresses what is fundamental to morality. In this chapter we shall begin the more detailed defence of the view by showing that respect for persons is the ultimate principle presupposed in our ordinary judgements of social morality.

The strategy of the chapter will be to begin by suggesting the partial truth of utilitarianism as a theory of public or social morality, and arguing that this theory hardly makes sense at all unless we presuppose that persons are to be respected. We shall then develop utilitarianism by showing how it can accommodate the existence of moral rules and social institutions. Ordinary moral judgements, however, lay stress on the concept of equality—there is a minimum equality of treatment which ought not to be overridden by any degree of social utility. Hence, we need to qualify our acceptance of the principle of utility by making room for a second principle of equality. Equality, however, also presupposes respect for persons, for the belief that a minimum equality of treatment is morally required depends on the prior notion that each person matters as an individual and so makes some claims which cannot be overridden. Ordinary moral judgements require us also to make room for a principle of liberty, which is roughly to the effect that the restrictions on a person's liberty which are morally permissible ought to be the minimum necessary for the maintenance of social utility and equality. The reason why ordinary moral views lay stress on liberty, we suggest, is that a person must have a certain elbow-room if he is to develop in himself those attributes which make him characteristically a person.

Our contention, then, is that an adequate theory of social

morality requires the three principles of utility, equality and liberty, and these, we maintain, all presuppose the principle of respect for persons as their ultimate justification. Alternatively, we may say that they are all the expressions of the attitude of *agape* in the face of the complexities of the organization of a social system.

2. UTILITARIANISM

It is one of the most generally agreed judgements of ordinary morality that unselfishness is to be commended and selfishness condemned. We can therefore say that ordinary moral judgements require us to make the ends of others our own by helping them to get what they want. This will include both a negative aspect—refraining from *interfering* with their pursuit of their aims—and a positive aspect of *co-operation*. It also covers the activity of helping them to avoid what they want to avoid, which can be called by the blanket terms of 'pain', 'distress', 'frustration', 'embarrassment'. Here again, helping people to avoid pain, distress or the like has a positive and a negative aspect: the negative aspect is not *causing* them pain or distress and the positive aspect is the taking of steps to *relieve* their pain or distress. But this gives us no clear guidance for action. For an action may relieve the sufferings of some while causing suffering to others, or we may be faced with a choice between different possibilities of action each of which will bring somebody something he wants. We therefore need a principle of action which would help us to decide what to do in such situations; and the principle which suggests itself at once is some version of the utilitarian greatest happiness principle. There are various ways of stating the principle, but let us make use of the most familiar, that of J. S. Mill:[1] 'Actions are right in proportion as they tend to promote happiness, wrong as they tend to promote the reverse of happiness.'

Now there is surely no point in organizing action to maximize happiness unless we think that happiness matters, and it is unintelligible to suppose that happiness matters without supposing that the people whose happiness is in question matter. But to say that they matter in this way is to say that they are objects of respect. Hence, the principle of utility presupposes that of respect for persons. Indeed, the requirements of ordinary morality which (we have just argued) give rise to the principle of utility are precisely

those for which the attitude of sympathy provides a natural motivation (as we saw in Chapter I, p. 24), and sympathy is an integral
part of the attitude of respect.

Instead of speaking of 'happiness' Mill could equally well have
used the language of wants and their satisfaction, and indeed would
have avoided a good many difficulties if he had done so. We may
therefore reword Mill's formula to fit what we have said so far
about the fulfilment of others' wants, and suggest as a guide to the
requirements of the principle of respect for persons the following
rule: 'The right action is that which fulfils the most desire' (includ-
cluding in 'desire' both desire to avoid things and desire to have
things, and calculating the amount of desire with reference both
to the numbers of people whose desire is fulfilled and to the
intensity with which they felt it).

The criticisms which might be made of this formula are almost
endless, but we shall concentrate mainly on those based on the
nature of moral rules (which will enable us to develop our theory
of social morality by bringing in the idea of institutional structure),
and on the claims of the principles of equality and liberty.

3. MORAL RULES

An objector to utilitarianism might say that although it may be true
in some contexts that we call those actions right which make for
the best consequences for the majority, in other contexts we seem
to call actions right or wrong simply because they are or are not
performed in conformity with moral rules. Thus, when we say, 'A
promise is a promise', we have not thought that keeping a promise
will lead to the best consequences for the majority; we simply issue
a reminder that there is a moral rule that one ought to keep one's
promise. Again, if a person has borrowed money it is right and
obligatory that he should return it simply because there is a moral
rule that debts ought to be paid. We do not say or think that a
person ought to pay back the money he has borrowed because this
will produce the best possible consequences for the majority; we
think he ought to pay it back because there is a moral rule that
debt-paying is obligatory. Indeed, there may be cases where the
consequences of paying a debt will be worse for all than those of not
paying it; yet we should still say that debt-paying is right. Suppose,
for example, that a person has borrowed £100 and that the lender

intends to squander the money in a selfish way when it is returned
while the borrower will use it in a worth-while way. The best
possible consequences for the majority would seemingly result in
this case if the money were not returned, and yet we should still
say that there is a rule that debt-paying is obligatory and that
therefore the money ought to be returned. The objection, then, is
that our ordinary views are not precisely reflected in the utilitarian
thesis that actions are right or wrong in so far as they produce the
best possible consequences for the majority; some actions may be
right for this reason, but we regard others as right simply because
they are instances of moral rules.

It is necessary in a reply to the objection to distinguish between
two possible ways of interpreting it. The first interpretation takes
the objection to be one of fact: that, as a matter of fact, we do not
always in everyday life refer to consequences when we are wonder-
ing whether acts are right or wrong. The second interpretation
takes the objection to be a conceptual one: that there is a conceptual
gap between the rightness of (some) actions and consequences,
and a conceptual link between the rightness of (some) actions and
moral rules. The second interpretation is the one which characterizes the deontologist's position. Let us consider the interpretations in more detail.

The first interpretation is reminding us that we often regard an
action as right simply because it is governed by a rule—of truth-
telling, promise-keeping, or the like—but it leaves open the
question of the connexion between rightness and consequences.
Now if the utilitarian can provide a justification for the existence
of rules it might seem that he can consistently meet the objection
so interpreted.

In his attempt to provide such a justification the utilitarian can
point out that we do not as individuals have the necessary
capacities to work out the consequences of all our actions. Our
experience is limited and our knowledge and understanding are
limited and we therefore cannot always work out the calculus of
consequences for ourselves, let alone for society as a whole. Moreover, supposing we could calculate the effects of our actions, we do
not always have time to do so before acting; we are often obliged
to make up our minds quickly on what is right or wrong, whereas
it would take time to go into the probable consequences of our
actions. Hence, the argument runs, moral rules have grown up

which express the accumulated wisdom of mankind on the consequences of action. Mill compares this function of moral rules to that of signposts or the *Nautical Almanack*: we have signposts to guide us across country which may be unknown to us.[2] Again, the sailor does not need to make his calculations at sea but goes to sea with his calculations already made for him in the *Nautical Almanack*, and similarly, we go across the sea of life with the consequences of our actions already calculated for us in moral rules. Thus, the utilitarian sees moral rules as being rules of thumb or ready reckoners which compensate for the deficiencies in the experience, knowledge, understanding and time of the individual person.

A utilitarian can also stress another function performed by moral rules. The nature of this function emerges if it is pointed out that in addition to the deficiencies for which 'lightning calculators' can compensate, human beings are also deficient in altruism and therefore require the threat of coercion to encourage them to seek majority interests rather than their own. The advantage of rules is that not only do they prescribe the types of action which are conducive to majority interest, their very existence helps to secure the compliance of most people. The reasons for this are, firstly, that habits of obedience and the desire to conform to established custom are deeply engrained in most forms of society, so that people will conform to a rule simply because it is a rule. Secondly, where the rules are basic to the continued stability of a society they may be incorporated in a legal system and supported by the threat of legal sanction, and also by the sanction of social approval and disapproval. Here then is another main function of moral rules—by their very existence, and by the legal and social sanctions which can be attached to them, they can reinforce behaviour patterns of proven utility. It may therefore seem that far from being an objection to a utilitarian view of the criterion of right action, such an interpretation of moral rules enriches the theory and makes it more accurately reflect our ordinary views.

But moral rules can be assimilated by the utilitarian theory only in so far as they are regarded merely as guides, as administrative rules to ensure that in view of human weakness the best possible consequences for the majority are in fact brought about. It is possible to argue, however, (and this is the second, the deontological, interpretation) that such a view of moral rules does not adequately reflect our ordinary views about them.[3] According to the utilitarian interpretation, moral rules are guides—signposts or almanacks—to help us calculate the consequences of our actions. But if we are ourselves lightning calculators it would seem on this interpretation of them that we are entitled to ignore rules, whereas our ordinary view is that we are not entitled to be cavalier about rules. Again, if for some reason of flood or landslide a signpost no longer points to the right route, we are entitled to pick our own route; and so it would seem that if for some reason keeping to a moral rule will no longer bring about the best possible consequences then we may, or perhaps should, ignore a rule such as that debts ought to be paid. But this, it may be argued, is precisely not our ordinary view, which is rather that debts ought to be paid regardless of the consequences. We may sum up the points of difference by saying that on the utilitarian interpretation the rightness of actions is necessarily connected with the production of the best possible consequences, and only contingently connected with moral rules, whereas on the rival deontological interpretation the rightness of some actions at least is necessarily connected with rules and only contingently, if at all, connected with good consequences. The objection of the deontologist—and it seems a valid one—is that, if the existence of moral rules admits of no justification other than the utilitarian one so far provided, we ought to have no hesitation at all about ignoring a rule if we think we can thereby bring about the best possible consequences; but this is simply not our ordinary attitude towards moral rules.

In reply, the utilitarian can point to the consequences of the conceptual gap between rightness and the production of the best possible consequences. If the deontologist is correct, it is theoretically possible that the performance of a duty could on a given occasion make the world a worse place than it would have been if the duty had not been performed. It might be argued that the very fact that a duty has been performed must mean that some good consequences will be brought about. But even if we grant that the mere fact of duty-performance is itself good, it still may be the case that the total state of the world after the duty-performance is worse than it would have been if the duty had not been performed. And if this is a consequence of the deontologist's interpretation of moral rules his interpretation must be rejected as a bad case of rule-worship. There are other objections to deontology, but this is the strongest, and the one which arises most directly from the utilitarian position. But, even if we grant that this utilitarian criticism of deontology is valid as far as it goes, the question still arises as to whether the utilitarian can answer the criticism made by the deontologist.

It may be said that he can, by distinguishing two different kinds of rules.[4] Some rules, he may contend, are, when all is said and done, only empirical generalizations about the results of types of action. Actions are not made right or wrong because of the existence of these empirical generalizations forbidding or enjoining them; rather we have the empirical generalizations because we have learned by experience that certain types of action are liable to have consequences which are morally bad or good. For example, 'One ought not to pass on malicious gossip' is a rule based on the fact that the transmission of malicious gossip can be misleading, hurtful or injurious to a person's reputation. It is not that any one case of malicious gossip is wrong *because of* the rule, for in judging the action as wrong in a given case one need not refer to the rule at all; it is simply that the rule provides safe moral guidance if one is in doubt. Again, it is often tiresome, irritating or hurtful to make a joke to someone about his appearance, and consequently one may make it a rule to avoid this line of witticism. But such a rule merely expresses what experience teaches; the wrongness of hurting a person's feelings in this way does not depend on the existence of the rule. The utilitarian can therefore recognize the existence of rules in the form of 'wise saws and modern instances', but the rightness or wrongness of the actions is established independently of the rules. Moreover, since rules of this type are only generalizations, they readily admit of exceptions—cases where an action of a kind which normally has bad consequences will have good consequences, and *vice versa*. When exceptions do occur we may abandon the rule without a qualm, since the rightness or wrongness of the action does not depend on it. The utilitarian may however add that we should be very cautious about assuming that any particular case is an exception, and perhaps leave a margin for error, as it were.

Other rules, however, have a different logical status. They are not empirical generalizations about the consequences of actions; rather they lay down the obligations inherent in some institution which is artificial in the sense that it owes its existence to rules. This is the case, for example, with rules that one should keep promises and with rules concerning property, such as 'Do not steal' and 'Pay your debts'; there would be no such things as promises, stealing or debts if there were not rules of conduct defining them. The rightness of promise-keeping or debt-paying and the wrongness of stealing can therefore be said to depend essentially on the existence of rules, and thus to be artificial, in that it owes its existence to the institution which defines the practice. Because of this, one can say that 'Promise-keeping is right' or 'Debt-paying is right' or 'Stealing is wrong' can all be in a sense analytic propositions: one could not explain the notion of promising, for example, without reference to the rule laying down the obligation to keep promises. But it should be noted that it is only *within* the institution (as it were) that 'Promise-keeping is right' etc. are analytic; there is presupposed a logically prior *synthetic* moral judgement that it is right that the given institution should operate. The utilitarian argument is that the operation of such institutions as a whole may be in the general interest even although individual instances of promise-keeping and debt-paying (say) may seem to be against it. We undermine the institution if we raise the question of interest in every case; the rules of the institution must be applied to preserve the institution. In this way the rules of institutions differ from empirical generalizations about the consequences of individual actions.

Now to say that the rules of institutions must be applied because they are rules sounds like an appeal to a new moral value of impartiality—'If you keep your promise to A, you must also keep it to B'. But in fact it is only a reminder that since we all benefit from the operation of the institution as a whole we are not justified in making exceptions to its rules simply because some bad consequences may result from keeping to them in a given instance. Rather, since the utility of the institution depends on continued trust in its operation, *any* departure from its rules is *prima facie* wrong and to be regretted. Here there is a contrast with empirical generalizations about consequences, which can be ignored without a qualm if a person can calculate the consequences more accurately for himself. To say that any departure from an institutional rule is *prima facie* wrong is not to say that exceptions are never permissible; but it is to say that an essential element in any calculation of the consequences of the projected exception must be the effect that making an exception will have on the status of the institution itself.

In other words, where the rule is that of an institution from which we all benefit, the consideration 'What would happen if everyone did it?' is morally relevant when an exception is mooted. No new moral value of impartiality is introduced simply by this consideration. And, in fact, as far as *moral* substance goes, rules such as 'Keep promises' actually incorporate a certain partiality or inequality. The promisee or the creditor is in a privileged position, and his claim overrides that of others concerned. We may say here that a man's position as promisee or as creditor gives him special *rights* which must be considered in preference to the majority interest; but that this inequality is justified in the majority interest.

The institutions of property and promise-making, with the rights and correlative duties bound up with these, are institutions in a rather vague and weak sense; the rules are not necessarily written down but are agreed upon by a kind of tacit consent. In any society, however, there will be many other institutions, some of a far more formal character. Indeed, viewed as a system, society consists not of an aggregate of individual persons but of a complex of institutions, such as businesses, factories, trade unions, schools, churches, military organizations, political and legal institutions, welfare organizations, banks and so on. An institution, in this sense, is a cluster of rights and duties with some social function, although, of course, it does not operate on its own but is operated by individual persons, who are vested with the rights and duties of the institution in which they operate. As before, the exercise of specific institutional rights or the performance of specific institutional duties will not be directly connected with the general welfare but obliquely so, *via* the operation of the institution as a whole. Thus, while it is not always apt to ask whether a specific institutional duty promotes the general welfare it is always apt to ask whether an entire institution, or the current form of it, does so.

These facts about institutions explain many judgements we make which at first sight go against the principle of utility. For example, we do not feel that a man is doing wrong in confining the area of his service to others to a small circle such as his immediate family and friends, although it might seem that the general interest would be better served if he did not merely consider a privileged group. The reason why we do not think it wrong is now clear; a man should consider his family in preference to others because he has special duties to his family and they have special rights against him;

a man is justified in 'taking on' these special duties because the institution of the family is (we may suppose) more conducive to the general interest than any viable alternative. A great many of the ordinary person's duties are institutional duties of this kind; the scope left to him for direct consideration of the general welfare (such as by charitable contribution of money or service) will be small. To say this (it must be repeated) is not to say that institutional duties *never* admit of exceptions; such a position would not be utilitarian and would smack rather of the rule-worship of which we accused the deontologist. It is to say that exceptions to institutional duties will be very infrequent indeed, since the connexion between the rightness of such a duty and the best possible consequences is oblique; the good consequences stem from the continued operation of the system as a whole.

We can now sum up our discussion by saying that it is possible to state utilitarianism in a way which does justice to our ordinary views on moral rules, provided we distinguish between empirical generalizations about the consequences of actions and institutional rules. Such a distinction enables us to incorporate the valid insights of deontology without committing us to the conceptual gap between rightness and good consequences which was the weak point of the theory. No crucial objection to utilitarianism can therefore be based on a consideration of the place of moral rules in our moral outlook. But a crucial objection can be based on an analysis of the concept of equality.

4. EQUALITY

So far we have suggested that rights are claims of privilege, asserting an inequality which, if justifiable at all, is justifiable in terms of majority interest. But is extreme inequality morally justified if it promotes the general welfare? If this were so, it would justify building the happiness of the majority on the sufferings of the minority.

An example of this would be a society where there are a few slaves in proportion to the free community, and it seems that the majority of society will be more prosperous under this arrangement than if the slaves are freed. We would, however, be likely to criticize this society, on the grounds that it is *unjust* or inequitable; it therefore seems that we judge such situations not only in terms of the amount of benefit but also in terms of the way the benefit is distributed, and may prefer a situation where it is reasonably equally distributed to one where the total of benefit is higher but the disparities between the best off and the worst off are great.

Utilitarians have often quite cheerfully admitted the need for the principle of equality, but have not seen that this means abandoning the claim that the principle of utility on its own can account for our views on the rightness of actions. Mill, for example, in his chapter on Justice in *Utilitarianism*[5] says that the dictum—'everybody to count for one, nobody for more than one'—expresses the principle of equality, and that it might be written under the principle of utility as an explanatory commentary. In a footnote he goes on: 'This implication, in the first principle of the utilitarian scheme, of perfect impartiality between persons, is regarded by Mr Herbert Spencer (in his *Social Statics*) as a disproof of utility to be a sufficient guide to right; since (he says) the principle of utility presupposes the anterior principle, that everybody has an equal right to happiness.' Mill, however, denies that the impartiality to which Spencer refers involves a second principle alongside that of utility. Impartiality, he says, 'is not a *pre*-supposition; not a premise needful to support the principle of utility, but the very principle itself. . . . If there is any anterior principle implied, it can be no more than this, that the truths of arithmetic are applicable to the valuation of happiness, as of all other measurable quantities.' In the passage quoted Mill seems to have missed the point Spencer was making. Thus he says that Spencer's account of the anterior principle to the principle of utility, that everyone has an equal right to happiness, 'may be more correctly described as supposing that equal amounts of happiness are equally desirable, whether felt by the same or different persons.' But this latter thesis, so far from being a mere re-wording of Spencer's, is surely incompatible with it. Mill's version allows the grossest inequalities in the way the happiness is *distributed*, whereas Spencer's does not. Bentham's dictum in itself seems to be ambiguous as between the two possibilities; but his general account of the felicific calculus is clearly compatible with inequality in distribution, and thus we may assume that his account does not incorporate equality any more than does Mill's thesis.

We have raised the question of equal distribution of benefit in connexion with an institution or system of rights and duties, but the same question can arise in connexion with the consequences of an individual action; it sometimes seems that the best consequences overall can be secured only at the price of the suffering of a few. Again, it seems that in judging such situations we take account not only of the total of benefit but also of the way in which it is distributed. In short, we judge consequences not only by a principle of utility but also by a principle of equality.

The principle of equality demands that any inequality in treatment must be justifiable in some way; the presupposition is that equal treatment is appropriate, and the onus is on him who discriminates to justify his procedure by pointing to some difference between the parties which affords a reasonable ground for discrimination. The concept of 'relevant differences' between people (differences which do in fact justify the discrimination being made) is thus an important one in connexion with equality.

It is in this context that the idea of universalizability can be introduced. There are really two distinct notions covered by the term 'universalizability', the logical and the moral, and these notions are employed in two distinct principles of universalizability. The logical principle concerns rules and reasons, and states that if a rule of action or reason for action applies to one case, it must apply to all similar cases. In other words, if one is applying a rule or acting for a reason no distinction of treatment may be made which is not based on some criterion of difference. This principle simply follows from the fact that rules and reasons are (at least by implication) *general* in scope. But it is of the greatest importance in connexion with the rule-following nature of persons. For human beings often justify their conduct in terms of rules and reasons; and in so doing they are logically bound to see those rules and reasons as justifying similar conduct by others in similar situations. (This indeed is part of what Kant meant when he spoke of men as legislating for others.*) This is not, of course, to say that rules apply without exceptions, but only that differences in application logically must be on *principle*—that is to say, they must really constitute qualifications in the original rule, rather than arbitrary departures from it.

As an example of the logical principle of universalizability, consider a rule like 'All young men must serve in the Army for two

* See Chapter I, pp. 21, 28.

D

years'. This rule as it stands applies to all young men. I cannot logically hold this rule and then say that it does not apply to some particular young man—unless I am prepared to explain what is different about him which exempts him (for example, poor eyesight) and thus in effect add a qualifying clause to the rule which could exempt others also. In other words, the rule becomes: 'All young men except those with poor eyesight must serve in the Army for two years'. This example shows how reasons are universalizable too; if I say 'This young man ought not to serve because he has poor eyesight' I am giving a reason which would apply to all other young men in the same situation.

The *moral* principle of universalizability is really a statement of the presupposition that equal treatment is appropriate. It may be expressed as follows: 'No distinction of treatment may be made which is not based on some *morally relevant* criterion of difference'. It thus requires that differences of treatment be not merely explained (as the logical principle demands) but morally justified. For example, I would satisfy the logical principle of universalizability if I gave as grounds for exempting certain people from the Army the fact that they all had blue eyes. But this fact is of no moral relevance. If on the other hand the criterion is something like 'being married' we can see why such a factor might be held to *justify* discrimination, not merely explain it.

Often the kinds of difference which are held to be morally relevant derive from the gap between equal treatment and equal satisfaction; if people differ sufficiently in need or capacity or situation they will not get equal satisfaction from equal treatment. For example, the married soldier's difference in situation means that treating him similarly to the unmarried soldier will not produce similar results in terms of happiness. But morally relevant differences may stem also from demands separate from equality altogether. Thus utilitarian grounds may justify a difference in treatment between some people and others, and so may grounds drawn from the principle of liberty. We shall shortly see how this happens when we discuss education as an example of the working of the principle of equality.

Difference in treatment is held by some to be justified also by difference in *desert*.[6] The notion of desert is the notion that how a man should be treated depends on his merits and demerits. These may be either moral or non-moral. Thus Aristotle, assuming that just distribution must be according to merit, suggests as possible candidates for merit free birth, noble birth, or wealth.[7]

Now opinions differ as to how far desert really creates a moral demand separate from those of utility and equality.[8] An extreme view would be that it is desert which is the primary value and that equality is not a separate value at all but is simply a corollary of a principle of desert. For if we have a principle that each should be treated according to his deserts, this implies that those of equal desert should be treated equally and those of unequal desert should be treated unequally, but it does not set up equality as an independent value. This seems indeed to be Aristotle's view.

But our current moral views seem rather to assign a comparatively small part in justifying inequalities to the notion of desert. This is especially so in the case of merits or demerits for which the possessor is not responsible, where we are apt to think that equality demands the rectifying of the imbalance rather than 'giving to him that hath'. Exceptions to this, such as 'He's a bright boy and deserves to succeed' are often to be seen as expressions of the principle of liberty rather than of desert.[9]

The principle of equality, then, is not absolute. We do not hold that all people must be treated equally in all respects, but rather that the claim of equality must be balanced against other claims. But at the same time we hold that there is a minimum claim of equality which *is* absolute. There are inequalities so extreme that they cannot be justified by appeal to the general utility or to any other value. This can be put another way by saying that each individual has rights to certain basic benefits (or at least to freedom from certain basic evils) which must not be infringed however far others would benefit thereby. The degree of inequality allowable will depend partly on whether those who come out of it badly choose or consent to it in some sense, and also partly on whether they (as well as the more privileged party) will be better off than they would have been under a more egalitarian arrangement (as may be the case for example with the paying of high wages as an incentive to acquire skills).

We can now see that even the moral principle of universalizability ('No distinction of treatment may be made which is not based on some morally relevant criterion of difference') expresses only one aspect of the principle of equality. To do justice to the demands of equality we must add another principle to that of moral universalizability, viz 'Extreme inequalities are not permissible on any grounds'.

We shall now discuss briefly some concrete examples of the interplay of the principles of utility and equality. Take first participation in government, which for most people is equivalent to voting.

We would normally say that everyone has an equal right to vote, and that differences such as the colour of a man's skin could not be relevant grounds for excluding him. The only criterion for relevance here is whether any fact about a man disables him from benefiting by the exercise of the right. This sounds at first sight as though we could exclude people from voting if they were sufficiently ignorant or unintelligent, on the grounds that such people cannot know what is in their interest and so the vote is of no use to them. But this would be a mistake. Voting is valuable not only for the benefits which the voter can win for himself by exercising his vote wisely. To be able to vote is a benefit in itself; the right to a say (however misguided) in matters which concern a man is demanded by respect for persons as self-determining creatures. One can indeed speak of a right to make one's own mistakes, and this is one instance of it.[10]

Education is another commodity which is good both in itself and in the further benefits which it brings. Here again the basic presumption is that everyone has an equal right to education. But educational resources, such as money, equipment and manpower, are in practice concentrated on two groups: those who are especially handicapped mentally or physically (and, if the Plowden recommendations are adopted, by their environment), and those who are especially gifted. These two types of 'positive discrimination' (to use Lady Plowden's expression)[11] can both be justified by the principle of respect for persons, but in entirely different ways. Thus discrimination in favour of the underprivileged is in reality an equalizing measure to reduce their handicap. Unequal *treatment* is needed to produce *results* which are not too unequal. On the other hand, discrimination in favour of the gifted is justified partly by the fact that they are especially capable of benefiting by extended education and partly by utilitarian considerations. The utilitarian justification is obvious; this is an example of a situation where everyone, not merely the privileged group, benefits from inequality. The justification in terms of difference of capacity is a more complex one and depends on an understanding of what kind of benefit education is. It seems to be valuable because it contributes to a particular kind of self-development—some would say the most important kind. (For a discussion of self-development see Chapter III.) Now one cannot speak of a right to equal self-development through education, since this type of self-development is not something of which everyone is equally capable. What we can say however is that everyone has a right to benefit as far as he is able from education, that equal capacities should be treated equally.

We can now see why the public school system is thought by some to be unjust—it gives educational privilege to those who differ neither in need nor in ability to benefit. But if we consider the chief arguments against abolishing it, we shall see the workings of another principle which is a very important part of respect for persons, that of liberty, or the right to do as one wishes unless it causes harm to others. This principle is important enough to need separate discussion and we shall turn to it when we have touched on the right to a minimum standard of living as a final example of the principle of equality.

Equality demands, not an equal standard of living for all, but a minimum redistribution of resources which ensures that everyone reaches a minimum standard of living. Greater equalization than this is ruled out partly by utility, partly by what appears to be an appeal to desert. Thus we think that giving everyone much the same standard of living whatever he does removes all incentives to work, and also constitutes an injustice to the industrious who 'deserve to succeed' while the lazy man 'deserves to fail'. Now in saying that the lazy man deserves to fail we are not necessarily condemning him morally. Rather we think that the lazy man may be deemed to have *chosen* a lower standard of living for the sake of a quiet life, and that if this seems to him the greater benefit we should not introduce what is in effect an *inequality* by allowing him to have it both ways. But not everyone would rather be poor than hardworking. Of course, people can also be poor through no 'fault' of their own but simply because they possess no talent of high market value; many a dustman would be a doctor or a dancer if he could. We still think, however, that it is justifiable that dancers and doctors should get more than dustmen, partly as an incentive to them to develop their talents, for which industry is needed, and partly because it seems right that by and large a man should be allowed to make what profit he can out of his talents. The first of these considerations appeals to utility, the second to the principle of liberty (which we shall discuss in the next section).

Before we sum up our argument so far let us consider two terms which often cause confusion in this context, namely, 'equity' and 'justice'. 'Equity' means roughly 'treating people equally when they should be treated equally, and differently when they should be treated differently'. Thus, equity is not the same as equality, and is quite consistent both with the view that equality has no independent claim, and with the view that there is a minimum independent claim of equality. Accordingly, it is not very informative to say that something is equitable; it does at least suggest however that due regard has been paid to the desert and the claim to equality of the *individual*, and that the issue has not been settled exclusively by an appeal to the expedient, which is of merely utilitarian value.

'Justice' can be used in two ways. It may refer to a man's rights under the specific institutions of a society, his institutional rights as we have called them. Or it may refer to deeper and more important principles in the light of which both institutional rights and the dictates of utility may be judged. These rights are those of equality and of liberty (which we shall discuss later). Justice, if it is conceived of in this more basic sense, is that which asserts the claims of the individual against the utilitarian claims of society. Because of this it is easy to think of justice as embodying respect for persons and of utility as hostile to it. But to think thus is to forget that the majority is made up of individuals. As Raphael says: 'By contrasting the claim of justice, as looking to the interests of the individual, with the claim of utility as looking to the interests of society at large, I do not imply that society is anything other than its members. In our practical deliberations, however, we often find it convenient to think of "the interests of society" as an abstracted entity, since we may know from experience that a course of action is likely to benefit or harm a number of members of our society, while not knowing which particular members will be affected on this occasion. The dangers of the abstraction are countered by the concept of justice, which emphasizes the claims of the individual as such.'[12]

We are now in a position to recapitulate the argument so far. Our burden has been that the principle of utility, in terms of the maximization of the satisfaction of desires, is related to ordinary moral rules in two distinct ways: rules can either be empirical generalizations about the best way to implement the principle, admitting of exceptions like other generalizations, or they can lay down men's duties and rights under some institution which can be justified as a whole in utilitarian terms. We compared this second type of rule to the duties and rights of various roles in the social system, and saw how in both cases rights were privileges giving their possessor a claim prior to that of utility. We then suggested another kind of claim which competes with and perhaps takes precedence over what one might call institutional claims, and modifies the claim of utility—namely, the claim of equality. This too can be expressed in the language of rights; it asserts the right of every man to some basic necessities, however much society at large might benefit by depriving him of them, and it further asserts the right of everyone to equal treatment in all respects unless the inequality can be justified by relevant differences. This demand for a minimum degree of equality in a system of social organization embodies the idea that each individual matters *in himself* as a person quite apart from any special features which may distinguish him. Hence, equality, no less than utility, presupposes the principle of respect for persons.

5. LIBERTY

We have so far suggested by argument and example that the principle of utility must be modified by one of equality if we are to have an account of public morality which reflects our ordinary moral attitudes, and that both these principles presuppose that of respect for persons. We shall now suggest that ordinary moral attitudes require us to modify the requirements of utility yet further by making room for another principle—that of liberty.

The principle of liberty states that it is wrong to curb people's desires unnecessarily, to interfere without justification in people's pursuit of objectives which are of interest to them. This principle seems especially germane to the principle of respect for persons, as the word 'respect' is often used in just this sense of 'tolerate' or 'refrain from interfering with'. The force of 'respect' in this sense is brought out by the example given by the Shorter Oxford Dictionary—that Louis respected the interests of his Protestant subjects. Again, in a characteristic passage, Hare tells us that what 'distinguishes the liberal is that he *respects* the ideals of others as

he does his own. This does not mean that he agrees with them—
that would be logically impossible, if they are different from his
own. . . . In saying that the liberal respects the ideals of others we
mean that he thinks it wrong to interfere with other people's
pursuit of their ideals just because they are different from his own;
and that he also thinks it wrong to interfere with their interests
merely because his own ideal forbids their pursuit, if *their* ideals
permit the pursuit of these interests.'[13] It is clear that the concept
of respect as non-interference is being used here, and it would be
possible to quote from other influential moral philosophers to
make the same point.

This notion of respect, in the sense of refraining from interference or regard for liberty, is the central theme of Mill's *On
Liberty*, and his main principle expresses it as follows: 'the sole end
for which mankind are warranted, individually or collectively, in
interfering with the liberty of action of any of their number is self-
protection. His own good, either physical or moral, is not a
sufficient warrant.'[14] Now what does Mill mean by 'self-protection'
here? To answer this, we must consider what was meant above by
'unnecessary' when we said that *unnecessary* interference with the
liberty of persons is wrong, and in the course of this discussion we
can show how liberty is related to equality and utility.

We have said that the principle of liberty declares that we ought
to be free to pursue objects of interest. But since human beings
tend to clash in their pursuit of objects of interest it is obvious that
complete liberty is self-defeating. The principle of liberty must
therefore be combined with the principle of equality, to produce the
conclusion that each person has an equal right to pursue objects of
interest; in other words, he may act at liberty to the extent that
every other person may do likewise. Thus, when Mill speaks of
'self-protection' he means that it is legitimate to forbid a person to
perform certain actions only if it can be shown that his performance
of them will interfere with the liberty of others.

How does the principle of liberty relate to that of utility? At first
sight the answer seems to be that liberty as governed by equality is
the same thing as the *negative* side of utility when governed by
equality. (The negative side of utility, as was explained at the
beginning of the chapter, consists in refraining from interference in men's pursuit of their aims and in not causing them pain
or distress.) It may therefore seem that the principle of liberty is

not an *independent* principle but simply an expression of one aspect of the principle of utility.

It can be shown, however, that the principle of liberty may conflict with the *positive* aspects of utility as governed by equality. These positive aspects stress the importance of achieving the maximum satisfaction of interests, and for this to be possible some degree of social co-operation is necessary. For instance, with a system of rules based solely on social harmony a person could be at liberty to seek medical help when he was ill; but it is only in a society with rules of co-operation that his seeking of medical help is likely to be materially effective. In other words, to have medical benefits it is necessary to have rules governing, say, taxation, and these cannot wholly be justified by the conception of social harmony but require also the concept of social co-operation to render their existence legitimate. Now such rules of social co-operation infringe people's liberty to do as they want, and we do in fact regard it as at least debatable how far individual liberty ought to be restricted in order to develop a system of co-operation in the interests of all. It is clear that there should be rules enforcing co-operation on matters such as health and hygiene, but how far beyond these matters a government or official body is justified in imposing further restrictions is a question which raises the issue of socialism versus *laissez-faire* individualism. It can be argued, for example, that the formal freedom to enter a university or to be employed is of no value. Freedom is worth having only if it is material, and it becomes a material freedom only when it is guaranteed by the state. The costs of this guarantee, however, are the restrictions with which anyone living in a socialist state is familiar. The price may be worth paying, but the point is arguable.

But what does 'worth paying' mean here? If the principle of liberty is simply one aspect of utilitarianism, the issue between (say) socialism and *laissez-faire* individualism amounts to no more than the question whether the greatest happiness is in fact achieved by not interfering with others and thus losing the benefits of co-operation, or by co-operating with others and thus losing the benefits of liberty. Now it is sometimes held that interest is maximized by a *laissez-faire* policy (though if we consider the need to meet the demands of equality this is perhaps an implausible view). But very often the point at issue is not how interest can be maximized. Most people would hold that it is worth *sacrificing* some measure of the general interest for the sake of a high degree of individual liberty. Thus the problem usually concerns the *degree* to which this should be done.

We can now see why the principle of liberty cannot in the end be identified with the negative aspect of the principle of utility. If it is admitted that the claims of liberty sometimes prevail over those of utility, then liberty, like equality, must be an independent value—one which cannot be accounted for solely in utilitarian terms. It remains to consider why we put this high value on liberty for its own sake.

We have said that to stress the importance of liberty is to stress that the area of his life in which a person is free of the restrictions of rules must be as large as is compatible with the existence of a similar freedom in the lives of others. The most plausible explanation of this stress is that we all recognize that freedom from external compulsion is necessary over a certain area of a person's life if he is to develop those attributes which make him characteristically a person. If a certain minimum freedom of action is violated by external compulsion then the individual will fail to achieve the level of self-realization which makes him a person: at first failing to express himself in characteristically human actions he will in the end fail even to envisage these actions as possibilities in his imagination. The principle of liberty is therefore the principle of respect for persons expressed in a context where the importance of self-realization is being weighed against that of achieving an harmonious and co-operative society.

It may be objected that the principle of liberty cannot be connected with that of respect for persons by insisting on the need for the human person to grow, because there is much evidence that this growth takes place in communities lacking in liberty. For example, in Scotland at the height of Calvinism there was little room for the expression of inclinations and ideals in the tight system of rules and regulations imposed by the Calvinists. Yet during this period, it may be argued, there was no sign of the human personality wilting away: on the contrary, it was a period of fierce individualism and independence in Scottish history. Hence, it may be said that liberty is not essential to the development of the human person, and consequently that the principles of liberty and respect for persons are only contingently connected.

In reply it can be argued, to begin with, that the restraints of Calvinism were self-imposed by the Calvinists. They were not the restraints of a secular state imposed from the outside, but were rather voluntarily adopted, and do not therefore offend against the principle of liberty. It was by means of the discipline of their restraints that Calvinists believed they were realizing what made them truly persons. Indeed, the importance of the principle of liberty to Calvinists is brought out if we consider how much they resented any interference with their liberty to be Calvinists. It is true that Calvin tended to impose suffocating regulations even on those who did not accept his beliefs, and that Calvinism stultified the artistic and cultural life of Scotland for hundreds of years. But this merely supports the point that enforced rules not connected with the maintenance of social harmony and co-operation kill human personality. Where Calvinism did lead to the growth of the human person its restrictions were freely accepted, and so were not felt as restrictions: but where they were externally imposed, and felt as restrictions, they did not lead to the development of the human person.

A fuller discussion of what is meant by self-development must be postponed till Chapter III. There, it will be noted, it is presented chiefly in terms of the way in which a man should respect humanity in his own person. This is indeed its chief importance. But we do have some duties to respect others' need for self-development and others' self-respect. Now these duties are mainly duties to respect another's liberty, as we have seen. To try to contribute to a man's self-development in some more positive way, by preventing him from indulging in the lower pleasures and forcing him to indulge in the higher ones, is a self-contradictory activity, as his own processes of choice are an important aspect of his self-development.

Two qualifications should, however, be added to this. When we are dealing with children we consider it legitimate to apply a certain amount of pressure on them to follow self-developing pursuits; for example, we think it right to compel them to be educated. We make an exception of children because we think they have not got the knowledge and experience to make any choice worthy of the name, and also because there are some talents which have to be cultivated young if at all, so that the adult's ability to make a valid choice (one with plenty of possibilities) itself depends on early restriction of liberty.

It might here be objected that if the restriction of a child's liberty is permissible in this way, we cannot speak of the *self-contradictoriness* of making a man indulge in higher activities for the sake of his self-development, as we did in the previous paragraph. But we may restrict the child's liberty only if this is in the interests of his own freedom later in his life. Thus we must not seek to indoctrinate him in such a way that he cannot later genuinely choose between one activity and another. It might also seem that what we have said about children would justify an over-paternalistic attitude towards childlike adults (primitive peoples for example) or even towards the less well educated who 'don't know what's good for them'. But the cases of the child and of the childlike adult are not similar. In the child we are endeavouring to develop the potentiality for choice in such a way that he can eventually take over. In the case of the childlike adult, however, we are not envisaging a time when he can take over, but are managing his life for him. And it is the span of the *individual's* life which counts—we cannot speak in terms of the childhood of a race and use this metaphor to justify treating its adults as children.

The second qualification is that we think that a government ought to subsidize the arts where there is not enough private patronage for them to be self-supporting. This involves using the money of those who are indifferent to the arts, and to that extent may seem to be an imposition of standards of worthwhileness on others. But there is a difference between imposing worthwhileness and making it possible. Money spent on the arts by the government makes worthwhileness possible for the few who desire it, and in so doing increases the range of possibilities for all, including those who are not interested. But the sums of money involved are too small to constitute an interference in the pursuit of whatever the individual chooses for himself. The Philistine would have a case against art subsidies only if he could plausibly maintain that his contribution restricted his area of choice rather than enlarged it.

We have said that liberty is to be valued not only for the sake of its possessor's interests, but also with a view to his self-development and self-respect. In discussing this we have partly answered a question which might be raised: how far making another's ends my own involves treating all his ends on a par. The answer seems to be that it is not for us to prevent him from pursuing ends just because we think them unworthy. But it may be legitimate to encourage some ends more than others. This does not, however, deal with the special case of a man's moral ends. Ought we not to regard these with special deference?

This is a very complex issue which we do not propose to investigate in detail here.[15] It arises most sharply when a man's moral convictions prevent us from carrying out some policy which we feel to be demanded on moral grounds. Are we justified in trying to get him to do what he believes to be wrong, by threats or bribes, for example—in other words, trying to corrupt him? Notice that this is not simply a question of taking his ends into consideration; rather the question is which of his ends should be regarded as paramount. And the question is not answered by declaring that a man would *rather* be bribed than overcome by force in some way. For even if in a given case this were his choice we can still ask whether such a preference is the right one, and thus again raise the question of the relative value of different types of end.

The conclusion of this discussion of liberty, then, is that ordinary moral views require us to modify the public morality of utility to make room not only for a principle of equality but also for one of liberty, and that the importance we attach to these principles in each case can be explained only if we assume that they are expressions of the basic principle of respect for persons.

6. FRATERNITY

WE have discussed liberty and equality at some length. What (it may be asked) of fraternity, which is so often linked with liberty and equality? Is there such a thing as a separate principle of fraternity? The answer seems to be that there is no one thing to which the term 'fraternity' unambiguously applies.[16] The best we we can do is to try to distinguish various possible meanings of the word and show how they relate to what we have so far said.

First of all, then, the term 'fraternity' may be applied to the policy of co-operation in the interests of all which, as we mentioned earlier, is apt to conflict with individual liberty. Thus we may say that in a communist state the principle of fraternity is exalted at the expense of that of liberty. Coupled with this may be a tendency to regard the community as an entity over and above the individuals which compose it, so that fraternity is held to demand the sacrifice of the individual to some abstraction such as 'the State'.[17]

Now this notion as it stands may be illogical, but at the same time it reflects a real deficiency in classical utilitarianism with its exclusive concentration on the individual. Thus writers like Mill do not make clear that a community is not merely an aggregate of individuals but has an institutional structure. How far this omission matters depends on whether Mill is thinking simply in terms of the whole of humanity from now to eternity as the field of reference from which the majority is drawn, or whether he is thinking rather in terms of present and future members of a particular community (the British nation?) which needs institutional definition to explain its continuity. If (as is likely) he is thinking of a particular community then his account is deficient in not explaining what constitutes a community such as a state. Those who think of the state as a self-subsistent entity have merely erred in the opposite direction.

The word 'fraternity' is also used sometimes to suggest something different in kind from a principle of social co-operation. It may stand for something more like the *spirit* in which rules should be applied. The force of this comes out when we consider what happens when the letter of the law is put into practice without its spirit and we have 'working to rule' with all that that implies. Even granting that 'working to rule' often means doing somewhat less than the rule indicates, we can still appreciate that for efficient operation of rules a certain 'spirit' is required which is something more than an administrative matter, even if it is less than an ideal of creative service. This spirit obviously involves a certain intelligence in the operation of rules, but more significantly it involves also a certain humanity.

The principle of fraternity so understood has to do with the need in society for a recognition of human fallibility in the pursuit of common social objectives. It does not refer to a set of rules but rather to a willingness to be of service where there are no rules and to a manner of enacting rules which speaks of the consciousness of a common human predicament. Such a spirit may be called one of 'co-operation', but co-operation in this context must be distinguished from the social co-operation which was equivalent to 'fraternity' in the first sense. 'Co-operation' or 'fraternity' in this second sense covers a host of detailed concepts concerned with our response to contingencies, with the quality of our enactment of social roles and with the manner of our adherence to and application of rules. For instance, fraternity in this second sense would cover concepts such as 'neighbourliness', 'tact', 'courtesy', 'discretion', 'give and take'. If we use the metaphor of social machinery we may say that fraternity in the second sense draws our attention to the need for oil.

So far, then, we have discussed fraternity as the *principle* of co-operation and as the *spirit* of give-and-take. A third meaning of 'fraternity' is again different in category. 'Fraternity' suggests above all a *motive* for action, a devotion of a kind resembling that felt to brothers but extended to the members of some community to which one belongs. In so far as people in a community really are imbued with a feeling of fraternity, they will not see restraints on liberty in the general interest as restraints—in fact they will not *be* such, but rather ways of bringing about what the individual wants most. This is the feeling which communism hopes to foster in its members. From motives such as these, people in a democracy choose to spend time in the service of others; and whereas it would be an infringement of liberty to *make* them do so, it is an exercise of liberty if they choose to do so.

It may be asked whether 'fraternity' is the same as 'respect' or '*agape*'. The answer to this question depends on the sense of 'fraternity' involved. Where fraternity is to be interpreted as a principle of social co-operation (our first sense) it simply amounts to another way of regarding one aspect of the principle of utility. As such it cannot wholly be explained in terms of *agape* for, as we have seen, the principle of utility is at best an imperfect crystal-lization of the attitude of *agape*. Fraternity in the second sense is similar to *agape* in that both concepts refer to a quality of response to people and situations which cannot be pinned down in precise rules. But *agape* is, of course, a wider conception than fraternity. Fraternity in the third sense—a motive for action within a com-munity—may or may not be explicable in terms of *agape*. If kinship is acknowledged only within some restricted group (of fellow-workers or the like) it is not the same as *agape*. But where fraternity can be expressed by a saying like 'The whole world is my kith and kin' it does seem to be the same as *agape*, where *agape* is regarded as a motive for action.

7. CONCLUSION

In our first chapter we investigated the attitude of respect for persons and suggested that it would give rise to the fundamental principles of morality, and in this chapter we have tried to show how this works out in detail for public or social morality. The theory of utilitarianism seemed at first to reflect our ordinary moral views since it suggested a detailed programme for 'making the ends of others one's own' in the life of a large and complex society. It turned out, however, that utilitarianism on its own provided only a distorted image of ordinary views and we had therefore to amend it to take into account the demands of the principles of equality and liberty. But the importance attached to the three principles of utility, equality and liberty can be explained only if we say that the principle of respect for persons is assumed. Our contention that respect for persons is the ultimate principle of morality is therefore justified to the extent that the ordinary judgements of social morality presuppose it. Fraternity turned out to be not an independent principle but (depending on its interpretation) a principle analysable in terms of utility or of *agape*.

CHAPTER III

RESPECT FOR PERSONS
AND PRIVATE MORALITY

I. THE PROBLEM

In Chapter II it was argued that our morality supplies us with rules of social organization all of which are to be explained in terms of the basic assumption that persons are to be respected as ends and never treated merely as means. Such an account may be said to describe morality in its social aspect.

The question can now be raised as to whether there is anything more to morality, or whether 'social morality' is really a pleonasm because morality is necessarily social in nature. Surely, it may be said, restrictions on behaviour which do not have a basis in some principle of social organization are to be regarded more as religious or conventional in nature than as moral. And such a view of the area of jurisdiction of morality would have the support of the utilitarian tradition in morality, this tradition being understood to include the dominant Anglo-Saxon fashions in moral philosophy at the present time. On the other hand, there are traditions which have seen morality as partly, or indeed as mainly, concerned with the development of certain qualities in the person himself. For example, it would seem that some Greek philosophers saw morality partly as a matter of the acquisition by the soul of certain virtues with a significance not fully explained by their social utility. Again, Christian ethics stress the importance of morality as a discipline to prepare the soul for a future life, and certain virtues emphasized in Christian teaching—humility and chastity, say—do not seem to admit of adequate analysis in terms of the principles of social organization. Finally, the Idealist movement of the nineteenth century saw the moral end as 'self-realization', and although the use of this term is not always clear in Idealist writings it at least suggests that Idealists found more in morality than its social aspect. Despite the prevailing contemporary orthodoxy, therefore, there is

E

no agreement among philosophers in the past as to whether morality is irreducibly social in nature or whether it also has a private aspect.

In this chapter we propose to argue (Sections 2-8) that there is a private aspect to morality,[1] and that it too presupposes as its ultimate ground the principle of respect for persons as ends (Section 9). We shall begin by considering some senses of the term 'private', for several of these are relevant to morality.

2. THE SENSES OF 'PRIVATE'

Firstly, we speak of 'private property'; but there cannot be a private morality in this sense. Another person can use my moral principles without being accused of theft or plagiarism. But to say that a person logically cannot own his moral principles is not to deny that in another sense his moral principles necessarily must be his. A person may well learn his moral principles from other people, but unless he consciously adopts them as his own then (at least on one philosophical view) it can be denied that he is regarding them as *moral* principles at all. On such a view there is a necessary connexion between 'being a moral principle' and 'being consciously chosen'; and what a person consciously chooses he can in one sense call 'his own'. But not all uses of the possessive make property claims: you can take 'my cold' and I shall not sue you. Hence, although there is a sense in which a person's moral principles logically must be his own, they do not thereby become 'private' in the sense in which property can be private.

Secondly, we speak of a 'private capacity', as contrasted with a 'public capacity'; and in this sense there can be a private morality. For example, we may contrast the strictness or laxity of a statesman's public morality with that of his non-official or private morality. Again, a man may wonder whether it is morally permissible for him to follow a certain policy in his public office of which he would disapprove in his private capacity. There are moral problems here, and perhaps philosophical ones as well, but they are not problems as to whether a private morality can exist or not in this sense. For clearly it can.

Thirdly, we speak of a matter as being one of 'private knowledge', as opposed to one of 'public knowledge'. 'Private knowledge' is here constrasted not with official knowledge but with general knowledge.

In a similar way we may contrast the morality of an individual person or small group with that which is publicly expected or required by the members of a community. The contrast involved here is often expressed in current writings as that between personal ideals and social morality. But where social morality is called the 'public morality' we can speak by way of contrast of the 'private moralities' of minority groups or single individuals within the community. It is once again clear that in this sense of 'private' there can be a private morality.

Fourthly, a person can have 'private thoughts', as distinct from those he publicly discloses. There can be a private morality in this sense, and it will be a pathological form of the previous one. A person's ideals may be such that he cannot publicly disclose them because they are at odds with the social morality of his community. For example, within a society there may be minority groups whose ideal it is to overthrow the existing order. Such people may go through the motions of accepting the public morality of their community while awaiting the revolution (or whatever). They can clearly be said to have a private morality because they do not disclose that they have these moral beliefs.

Fifthly, a man can have a 'private secretary' who is concerned exclusively with his affairs, and in this sense 'private' can mean 'that which is individual or personal, that which concerns oneself alone'. Can morality be 'private' in this sense? The question is ambiguous. In the first place, it may be asking whether all moral duties or evaluations are necessarily public in the sense of 'universalizable', or whether a man might be said to have a duty or to make an evaluation which was private in the sense that it referred only to himself and not to all other people in similar situations. The question so interpreted raises the familiar philosophical problem of universalizability. But this is not the problem we shall be discussing here.* For even supposing we allow that it is intelligible to speak of a duty or a moral evaluation which applies only to the agent himself, it can still be the case that this duty or evaluation may concern his relations with others. Captain Oates, for example, may have felt that what he ought to do was not universalizable, but his action was none the less intended to benefit others, and was so far a matter of *social* morality.

---

* We have already indicated a view on universalizability in Chapter II, and shall discuss it further in Chapter V, Section 1.

The question to be raised is rather that of whether there can be a morality, or an aspect of morality, the object of which is the agent himself, which is private in its scope or what we may call 'self-referring'. Such a morality, if it exists at all, will be universalizable; its duties will not simply be duties for a given nameable individual (if such a conception be intelligible) but duties for a man as such, or so at least we shall argue. The *content* of the duties, however, will be concerned with the nature of the agent himself and not with other agents or society at large. For this reason such a morality, if it existed, could be called a 'private morality'; and the problem of whether or not it exists is a philosophical one, for it raises questions about the scope of the concept of morality.

3. CURRENT VIEWS

A good deal of current moral philosophy is written with the assumption that all morality properly so-called is public or social morality. Some philosophers are explicit on this. For example, Dr David P. Gauthier writes that 'moral problems are never merely the concern of the agent confronted by them; moral problems necessarily involve the interests of others'.[2] Again, Professor D. D. Raphael writes that '. . . in speaking of obligatory acts I have said that their content always relates to the *interests* of other persons or creatures'.[3]

Other philosophers are less certain, or at least less explicit. For example, Professor P. Nowell-Smith writes[4] that although we cannot strictly *define* duty in this way '. . . it has always seemed natural to represent duties as the demands made on us by others'. It is true he also writes that if 'we thought that a man was ruining his life by excessive abstinence, we might well say that he ought to pursue pleasure more than he does'. But the 'ought' here cannot (presumably) be a moral 'ought', for we are told that 'moral codes never contain injunctions to people to pursue their own pleasure. . .'. His position seems to be that moral and non-moral obligations are alike in presupposing disinclination to perform the actions considered obligatory, and in stemming from rules which co-ordinate interests. But whereas non-moral obligations stem from rules which co-ordinate one's own interests, *moral* obligations stem from rules which co-ordinate the interests of other people *with* one's own. And this position is similar to that of Gauthier or Raphael.

Another approach is that of Professor P. F. Strawson. In his paper 'Social Morality and Individual Ideal'[5] he distinguishes between a sphere of morality (which is social) and one of individual ideal (which need not be). Now it might be said that what we are calling 'private morality' can be located within the sphere of individual ideal—a sphere which Strawson refers to (ambiguously) as that of 'the ethical'. But it is doubtful whether anything properly to be called morality is to be located in this sphere, for individual ideals are said by Strawson to 'captivate', to be 'appealing' or 'attractive', or to represent the 'nobleness' or 'sanctity' of life, whereas morality, as we shall later attempt to establish, is a matter of *obligation*.* Even if we adopt this 'two-tier' approach to morality, then, the moral element properly so-called seems to be social or public.

The explanation of the similarities in the positions of these writers (who are characteristic of contemporary secular moral philosophy) is that they all share the liberal approach to morality— the approach which was given its classic statement in Mill's *On Liberty*.[6] If a philosopher thinks (if we may quote the passage again) that the 'sole end for which mankind are warranted, individually or collectively, in interfering with the liberty of action of any of their number, is self-protection', then he will see morality as necessarily social in nature—as a matter of harmonizing the interests of people on a co-operative basis. *Logically* speaking, of course, he is not committed to this position. It is possible to hold both that one's duties to others are confined to the sphere of harmonizing interests (that one has no duty or right to 'improve' them) and that one has duties to oneself. Indeed, one might rest one's views on the rights of others to non-interference on a belief that it was their duty to choose to develop themselves (or whatever) not one's duty to make them. And this, as we shall see, may in fact have been the position of Mill in *On Liberty*. *Historically* speaking, however, the influence of *On Liberty* has been to encourage philosophers to see morality as social in nature. This is the explicit position of Gauthier and Raphael. It is compatible with this position to add that a man may make rules for himself to harmonize his own long-term interests (the position of Nowell-Smith) or that

* See Section 6.

he may be attracted by various ideals of the good life which need
not concern others (the position of Strawson). None of these
positions allows us to speak of a morality which is private in the
sense of 'self-referring'.

4. PRIVATE MORALITY AND THE VIRTUES

Historically, various concepts have been used as the nucleus of
attempts to articulate the nature of private or 'self-referring'
morality by those who believed in its existence. For example, some
philosophers have seen obligations as arising out of the conception
of what it is 'natural' to do, and what it is 'natural' to do was not
thought to be exhausted by what it is socially useful to do. Others,
and particularly Kant, have tried to base a private dimension of
morality on the concept of self-respect—a concept interpreted as
being analogous to the respect in respect for others. We shall begin
by examining our attitudes to certain virtues. Take first the virtue,
or alleged virtue, of prudence.[7]

Prudent action is certainly concerned essentially with the agent
himself and is therefore private in the relevant sense. Moreover,
it has traditionally been said that prudence is a virtue and
imprudence a vice. Hence, prudence seems to be a duty of private
morality.

In assessing this argument a critic might maintain that the judgement that prudence is a virtue is only a loose form of speech, for
imprudence is a neglect of one's own interests and such a neglect
is a piece of foolishness rather than of wrong-doing. But this assess-
ment is inadequate, for there is more to our condemnation of
imprudence than the judgement that the agent in neglecting his
interests is simply being silly. There are in fact two components in
our adverse judgement on imprudence: the 'interest' component
and the 'rationality' component. In neglecting his interests the
agent is failing to achieve benefits for himself to which there is no
moral obstacle, or is even harming himself. This is not as such
morally wrong (many would argue). But in failing to achieve
benefits for himself to which there is no moral obstacle, or in
harming himself, the agent is also being *irrational*, and it may be
argued that there is a duty to act rationally. For, as we have
argued in Chapter I, a man's reason is constitutive of his nature as
a person, and it may be said that we have a duty to respect the

human nature we have in common, or to act as a person. This
provides us with a clue to the nature of private morality.

Consider next the virtue of courage. Courage is a disposition
which enables a person to do what it is reasonable to do in the face
of fear. Similarly, the temperate person is able to do what he has
most reason to do when he is faced with the temptation of pleasure.
It may be argued that to respect oneself as a person is to develop
such virtues. It is true, of course, that there is utilitarian justification for cultivating the virtues, but our claim is that more is required for their adequate analysis, and that this 'more' throws into
relief an area of morality which concerns the individual's conduct
in respect of himself.

Take the case of the person who is guilty of cowardice. Such a
person may blame himself in that his cowardice has brought injury
to others, but he may also blame himself for another reason as
well; he may feel that in some important respect he has failed as a
person, as a human being. The point emerges more clearly in the
case of intemperance. The intemperate man may bring harm on
others or on himself, and in different ways be blameworthy for
these reasons. Suppose, however, that his intemperance does not
interfere with his business occupations and that it can somehow
be confined to the solitude of his own home; he has performed his
public duties, but his private desires are all for an intemperate
mode of life. Now if it is true that all morality is social morality,
then such a man will escape the net of moral censure. Our claim,
however, is that it would commonly be said that there is something
morally wrong in the situation, and that we require the use of a
concept other than that of social morality or of self-interest to
analyse it adequately. The concept needed is that of private
morality—that aspect of morality which is concerned with a
person's duties to behave as a human being, regardless of the
utilities of acting in such a way.

5. PRIVATE MORALITY AND SELF-REALIZATION

We shall now approach the notion of private morality from another
direction by investigating the concept of self-realization or self-
development. In recent decades the term 'self-realization' has not
been seen much in the writings of professional philosophers of the
Anglo-Saxon tradition. This has been due partly to the eclipse of

nineteenth-century Idealism, which made 'self-realization' a key-term of its moral philosophy and bequeathed it as a slogan to our ordinary vocabulary and moral conceptions. It is due also to the wet, squashy appearance of the concept with its suggestion of something unsuitable for dissection by the precision instruments of contemporary analytical philosophy. Nevertheless, the concept, and even the term itself, do continue to haunt the pages of writers on education and social work. And interested laymen invariably regard it as a term which seems to point to something important and deserving of further articulation.

If the concept is to be given the slim lines which appeal to modern tastes it cannot be discussed in terms of Idealist philosophy. This is not because the Idealists had nothing to teach us of relevance to understanding our moral outlooks, but because the Idealist moral *kerygma* is so hard to disentangle from the myths of their metaphysics. An historical context is useful as a basis for a general discussion, however, and one is provided—somewhat surprisingly—by J. S. Mill. Mill's name is generally associated either with the hedonistic doctrines of *Utilitarianism* or with the liberal approach to morality to which we have already referred, but in the third chapter of *On Liberty* he suggests a conception of the moral end in terms of self-realization or (as he calls it) self-development.[8] We shall not give a detailed or systematic account of what Mill actually says, but shall merely use his writings as material for developing a theory of self-realization in so far as this has bearing on the nature of private morality.

One view of self-realization which emerges from Mill may be called the 'complex objective' view. He tells us (quoting Wilhelm von Humboldt) that the end of man is 'the highest and most harmonious development of his powers to a complete and consistent whole'. Now to develop those powers we require to pursue certain objectives in our lives. Thus, it may be said that we shall realize ourselves if we pursue ends which are rich and complex and therefore suitable for bringing out and developing the potentialities that are within us. On this view, we ought to pursue poetry rather than pushpin; poetry will impinge on a greater area of our lives than pushpin and will therefore be an appropriate vehicle for developing those things in us which are characteristically human. It is true that there are many people who *prefer* pushpin to poetry, but (Mill would say) they are dull, shallow people whose individuality has never been developed. As Mill himself puts it, 'It really is of importance not only what men do, but also what manner of men they are that do it'.[9]

This view of self-realization contains obvious truths, but it is open to criticism and is inadequate as it stands. It may be argued, for example, that it is unrealistic if it is intended as a statement of an aim everyone can adopt. Persons who are no more than average in intellectual ability and education—not to mention those who are below this level—are simply not able to appreciate 'complex objectives' as described. To oppose poetry to pushpin as if they were a realistic pair of objectives is to reveal a lack of awareness of how far a genuine appreciation of poetry (say) is from the average and below-average capability. The criticism, then, is that many people have neither the desire nor the ability to appreciate 'complex objectives', and it is therefore not plausible to give the concept of self-realization such an interpretation if it is to be of help in analysing the nature of private morality.

This criticism can be avoided by a second view of self-realization, also to be found in Chapter III of Mill's *On Liberty*. The second view is that self-realization is to be attained by the *conscious* and choiceful pursuit of an object of interest to the agent, whatever that object may be. On this view, the stress is on 'being oneself', as opposed to 'conforming to custom'. To say this is not to say (Mill would argue) that people should ignore the experience of others or that they should ignore or depart from the customs prevailing in their society, but that whatever they do should be done consciously and deliberately as something chosen by the agent himself because he wants to do it. A custom may be a good one, but as Mill puts it, 'to conform to custom merely *as* custom does not educate or develop [in a person] any of the qualities which are the distinctive endowment of a human being'.[10] Mill seems to equate self-development in this sense with 'being original', but this is intelligible if we assume that no two people are quite alike, so that to be oneself is to be not quite like anyone else, and in this sense 'original' or 'an individual'. Existentialists, while they would scorn the term 'self-realization', would nevertheless agree with the doctrine to the extent that they see man's good as lying in the authentic choice of ends, whatever they may be, and his chief, or indeed his only, evil as lying in *mauvaise foi*, or the blind conformity to custom. On the second view, then, to realize oneself is to pursue any objective, provided one does it from choice and with one's heart in it.

The second view—the 'conscious choice' view—contains, like the first, obvious elements of truth. To realize oneself it is clearly necessary to *be* oneself, and this would be precluded by blind conformity to prevailing fashions. But again, like the 'complex objective' view, the 'conscious choice' view is an oversimplification. Certain objectives are more rewarding than others, and if a person chooses one of the less rewarding, then, whether the choice is conscious or not, he is not going to develop himself to the utmost as a result. Even if the appreciation of poetry is not a realistic objective for most people, it is also true that they are not going to achieve self-realization as a result of the choiceful pursuit of pushpin. Some compromise must therefore be found between the first and the second of the two views; and a clue to the compromise is provided by the phrase of Mill's which we introduced in Chapter I—'the qualities which are the distinctive endowment of a human being'.

Mill does not provide us with a detailed account of those distinctive qualities, but after speaking of the 'distinctive endowment of a human being' he goes on to write that the 'human faculties of perception, judgement, discriminative feeling, mental activity, and even moral preference, are exercised only in making a choice'. We may assume that his list contains what he considers the 'distinctive endowment' to be. It is now possible to combine the two views of self-realization by saying that it will be attained by the deliberate pursuit of ends which bring into use those 'faculties', to the extent that the agent possesses them. The extent will obviously vary enormously, but the 'faculties', as Mill stresses, can all be improved by use. Moreover, they are to some degree the possession of every normal human being since they are the 'distinctive endowment' of a human being, and constitute the generic human 'self'.

Let us assume that the concept of self-realization can be given content in roughly the manner indicated, and that the conduct it enjoins is 'private' in the relevant sense. The crucial question which remains is whether the conduct is enjoined as a matter of morality or only of self-interest.

If we accept the view of morality presented by the contemporary secular orthodoxy in moral philosophy—the view illustrated in

Section 3—then we cannot regard self-realization as a concept of morality. Morality, according to the prevailing view, is mainly (or is even necessarily restricted to) a matter of harmonizing the interests of people on a co-operative basis. It is concerned with the impact we make on other people and with ensuring that each person obtains the maximum satisfaction of his interests compatible with every other person's doing likewise. On such a view, self-realization cannot be a concept of morality since it is not concerned with our conduct *vis-à-vis* other people, but with our conduct *vis-à-vis* ourselves. It may be said, then, that if self-realization is not a concept of morality it must be one of self-interest; the justification for commending self-realization being simply (in Mill's terminology) that it will produce more pleasure for the 'self' concerned. To commend an activity because it involves the choiceful employment of distinctive human qualities and is therefore conducive to self-realization is simply a roundabout way of saying that it will produce a greater quantity of pleasure to certain people over a long period.

Now it is not necessary to deny—and certainly Mill would not deny—that a person in the process of developing his potentialities is also likely to experience on the whole a greater quantity of pleasure than one who simply conforms to convention. But the justification for stressing self-realization does not lie in the pleasure which may accompany its attainment. Nor does Mill think it does, for he provides justification of another sort. He writes that human nature 'is not a machine to be built after a model . . . but a tree, which requires to grow and develop itself on all sides, according to the tendency of the inward forces which make it a living thing'.[11] Again, he praises the 'Greek ideal of self-development' and suggests that if human beings develop what is individual in themselves they will become 'a noble and beautiful object of contemplation'. In these and other passages Mill seems to be working with a conception—partly moral and partly aesthetic—of human nature as something which may, more or less, 'flourish'. The argument, which is at least as old as Socrates, is that it is somehow expected or required of us as human beings to act in ways which will make our human natures 'flourish'. This is what Mill seems to have in mind when he stresses self-development, and although it is not clearly worked out in his thought, the conception does not appear to be hedonistic, nor one of self-interest. Rather it is a moral concept; not of the morality which regulates our social behaviour, but of that which, more vaguely, suggests what is incumbent on us as human beings. We wish to argue that this incumbency constitutes the core of private morality.

6. PRIVATE MORALITY AS OBLIGATORY

An argument to support this contention might be based on the premise (which we shall defend in Chapter V, Section 1) that only a duty can override a duty. Let us consider the case of an unmarried daughter who debates with herself in all sincerity whether she ought to develop some distinctive quality—say, an artistic gift— or to devote herself to caring for her aged parents. (We shall assume that the two are not compatible.) Now it may be said that any hesitation she has in deciding what she ought to do must mean that she is balancing her own interests against those of her parents (for we shall exclude issues of the possible social utility of her artistic gifts). But if the girl sees the situation as involving, on her side, nothing but her interests (that is, her likes and dislikes), then her hesitation in deciding what she *ought* to do cannot be sincere; for a duty cannot be overridden by an interest, and clearly consideration of her parents' interests constitutes a duty. Hence, if we assume that there could be a situation in which such hesitation would *be* morally sincere, we must interpret the hesitation as implying the recognition of a duty to develop distinctive human qualities. And if we assume the further premise (which again will be defended in Chapter V, Section 1) that all overriding claims are *moral* claims, then we can conclude that the duty to develop distinctive human qualities is a duty of private morality in the relevant sense.

Now even if it is admitted that this argument creates some approving response in our moral consciousness, a critic may suggest that private morality in this sense is also private in the third sense. In other words, while allowing that some people may recognize duties to develop their distinctive human endowment, a critic may suggest that such duties arise out of particular *ideals* of the good life, and he may go on to maintain that they are less basic than the duties of public morality, that they are, so to speak, 'optional extras' of the moral life.

But what does 'less basic' mean here? It may mean, in the first place, 'less obligatory'. But is this an intelligible conception?[12] Can a moral 'ought' be more or less of a moral 'ought'? It might be said that if there is a conflict between two obligations, A and B, and we decide that we ought to perform A rather than B, we have *ipso facto* decided that A is a stronger obligation or that it is more obligatory; and to decide in this manner is to show that we can give a sense to 'more obligatory'. But this argument is confused. Where there is a conflict between two incompatible actions, only one of these actions can strictly be called an obligation. It may well be that we have, in general, obligations to tell the truth, say, and to keep promises; but in a situation where we cannot do both, and we decide we ought to do one rather than the other, we have, strictly speaking, no obligation at all to do the other. Hence, we cannot say that one is more obligatory than the other, since the other is not demanded at all in the situation.

But it may be argued that some general *types* of action are more obligatory than others. For example, it may be said that while there is in general a duty to relieve pain and a duty to produce happiness, the former type of duty is 'more obligatory' in the sense that any action of that type will, on any given occasion, have a prior claim relative to actions of the latter type. Now it might be replied that the difference between the duty to relieve pain and the duty to promote happiness is that the former type of duty is more conducive to what is taken to be good than the latter; and that 'being more conducive to what is good' does not mean 'being more obligatory'. Suppose, however, that a critic (a utilitarian, perhaps) persisted in maintaining that 'being more conducive to what is good' was precisely what he did mean by 'being more obligatory'. It still would not follow that the distinction between the more and the less obligatory would always reflect the lines of the distinction between public and private morality; for, as perhaps in the case of the unmarried daughter, *sometimes* a duty of private morality can override one of public morality. Hence, even if we allow that a sense can be given to 'less obligatory', it does not follow that private morality is 'less basic' in this way.

It might be replied that we have been assuming that the requirements of private morality are *obligatory*, whereas they in fact represent what is simply a 'morally good thing'. Certainly (the argument may go on), it is better that a man should act according to private morality than that he should not, but this 'being better than' does not amount to a moral *duty* in the full sense. In this way, private morality is 'less basic' than public. Now we could reply to this point by using once again the premise that only a duty can override a duty and restating the example of the daughter which (we claimed) illustrated that private morality can give rise to duties in the full sense. But the point can be met in a different way by asserting the position that either a claim constitutes a moral *obligation* or it is not a moral claim at all. It is true that an agent may say, 'It is better that I should do A than B' or, 'It is better that I should do A than not', but if he admits that by 'better' he means '*morally* better' then he has admitted he has a *duty* to do A. And if 'better' does not mean 'morally better' then there is no moral obligation laid on him at all. It is true, of course, that we may be hesitant about using the *word* 'duty' of whatever a person thinks he ought to do. 'Duty' is tied in ordinary usage to what can be reasonably expected of a person, and if a person fails to act in a heroic way we are disinclined to say that he has failed in his duty, whatever *he* may think of himself. This seems to be the main point of Mr. J. O. Urmson's 'Saints and Heroes'.[13] But it does nothing to upset our contention that what a person sees as a moral claim on himself he sees as *obligatory*. Hence, if it is admitted at all that private morality is *morality*, then it is *ipso facto* admitted that it is obligatory, and, in that sense at least, on a par with public morality.

But a third meaning may be given to 'less basic'. It may be argued that a private morality in the sense outlined is an *ideal* which a man may or may not adopt at will. It is true, the argument may concede, that if a man does adopt it as a moral ideal, then it becomes *for him* something obligatory. But there is no obligation to adopt such an ideal. In a similar way, *if* a man becomes a Christian (say) he will look on a number of actions as morally obligatory which a non-Christian may see differently. But there is no duty to be a Christian. In this sense, it might be claimed, a private morality is 'less basic' than social morality, which a man *must* adopt to the extent that he lives in society.

The first step in answering this objection is to deny that a private morality presupposes any specific set of beliefs such as one may find in a religion; a private morality (as we are using the term) is not a specific ideal which a man may or may not adopt according as he is or is not attracted by it. Awareness of the claims of private morality (and this is the second step) arises along with self-conscious awareness of oneself as a person; and if one cannot avoid the claims of public morality to the extent that one is a person in society, then, *a fortiori*, one cannot avoid the claims of private morality to the extent that one is a person. We shall try to develop this argument by considering the sense in which moral claims can arise out of self-conscious awareness of oneself as a person.

The idea has already been introduced in Chapter I by means of the Greek notion of an *ergon*. The significance of a craftsman, as we pointed out, was thought to reside in his function as a craftsman, and his particular virtue in being a good craftsman. This notion we found to be extended, in Aristotle for example, to apply to a man himself. The idea is that there are certain forms of activity which a man, by having the nature he does have, is best fitted to perform; and his virtue is in performing them. This is not simply the idea that it is in a man's interests to act in certain ways, but also that it is fitting and proper that he should act in these ways, ways which express his nature as a person. Such ideas are developed in Christian thinking and in Natural Law doctrines.

Now it is obvious, as we argued in Chapter I, that the conceptions of a 'person' or 'human being' or 'man' which are employed in this discussion are already evaluative. From the totality of the human biological inheritance certain features are being picked out as central to the concept of a person, and it is the development of these rather than of others which is thought to be the concern of private morality. To some extent the features selected as crucial will vary according to cultural conditions, although it is easy to exaggerate the extent to which this is so. Are there, for example, societies in which it is thought wrong to be courageous, or in which the development of artistic gifts is frowned upon? There may be, but it is not easy to see how they could survive long without modifying themselves. But even supposing we concede that the precise nature of the claims of private morality will be culturally conditioned, depending on the view adopted as to the nature of a person, it is still arguable that in no culture is it a matter of moral indifference what sort of person one makes oneself. It is therefore not possible to disregard the claims of private morality any more than it is possible to disregard those of public morality. In this sense, then, private morality is not less basic than public.

But there is a fourth sense in which private morality might be said to be 'less basic' than public. It might be said that without the social stability provided by public morality, private morality could not exist, and in that sense it will be 'less basic'. But it is true only to a limited extent that private morality cannot exist without public. It is true to the extent that where there is social instability, or where society exists in only a rudimentary form, a person may find it hard to cultivate in himself certain human qualities, or indeed he may not be fully conscious of the possibility of their development as human qualities. This may be true of artistic gifts or of gifts for theoretical speculation, which seem to require a measure of social stability and sophistication if they are to flourish. But these by no means exhaust characteristic human qualities. During times when public morality has broken down, or hardly exists, a man will still have duties to behave with courage, temperance and dignity, and we approve of his conduct not solely for its social utility (or so we claim) but also as an example of human nature 'flourishing'. Hence, it is only to a limited extent true that in this fourth sense private morality is 'less basic' than public. And in no sense can we say that private morality is an 'optional extra' of the moral life.

7. PRIVATE MORALITY AND DUTIES TO SELF

It might be objected to the conception of private morality that it depends on a notion which can be shown to be unintelligible, namely the notion of duties to self. The argument that the concept of duties to self is unintelligible begins from the premise that the existence of a duty to a person requires that the person has a right correlative to the duty such that the right-holder may or may not, as he wishes, demand performance of the duty. But (the argument goes on) one and the same person logically cannot have both a right and its correlative duty in this sense; and if the conception of private morality leads to this contradiction then there must be something defective in it.

We have no need to accept this conclusion, however, for the initial premise on which it is based is open to criticism. Helpful in this context is a discussion by Professor Bernard Mayo.[14] Mayo reminds us that there is a traditional distinction between duties the discharge of which (1) involves, (2) does not involve, a specific person or persons. Mayo subdivides (1), namely, duties the discharge of which involves a specific person or persons, into (1a) duties which arise from undertakings, and (1b) duties which do not arise from undertakings. As an example of (1b) he takes the case of a person who has a duty to rescue a drowning child. It is clear that this could be a duty, but it is equally clear that the child cannot be said to hold a right against the rescuer. In this sense we can have duties concerning specific persons without having to say that these persons have rights against us. The correlativity of rights and duties holds only for (1a), and it is only in this category that we need to speak of duties *to* someone, as distinct from duties concerning someone.

Applying this argument to the question of whether we have duties to ourselves we have two ways of describing the situation. We can deny that we have duties to ourselves—for we have given no undertakings to ourselves—and assert that our duties are *concerning* ourselves (but not owed *to* anyone). Alternatively, we can allow that we do have duties to ourselves, but point out that 'to' does not here indicate a person to whom the duty is owed, but rather the sphere in which it is performed. We have in fact been arguing that there are duties *to do* certain things—to develop our human nature—and these duties are 'to' ourselves only in the sense that we, rather than other people, are their location. That is why we are calling them duties of private morality.

8. PRIVATE MORALITY AND EGOISM

It might be objected that what we are calling private morality is in fact a form of egoism. The objection can adopt a less or a more radical approach. The less radical approach is based on the premise[15] that the enlightened moral consciousness has a bias towards others, and the charge is that the alleged existence of private morality seems incompatible with this premise. For example, the altruistic bias in our moral consciousness might require us to help someone else—require us to make his ends our own—and (the argument goes on) the fulfilment of such a requirement might on occasion compromise the fulfilment of the demands of private morality.

In reply to the objection it can be said that altruism requires only that our own *interests* or *inclinations* give place to those of another person, but private morality lays down no duties to follow our own inclinations or pleasures; such an idea is indeed logically odd (as Nowell-Smith pointed out). Rather, private morality

F

requires us to develop characteristically human qualities, and even where this policy conflicts with helping another person the issue of altruism does not arise, because the conflict is not one between our own *inclinations* and those of another person. It is not obvious (as we argued in the case of the unmarried daughter) that a duty to develop a gift ought always to give way to a duty to further someone else's interests; but in any case this is not the issue of altruism versus egoism.

But the charge of egoism can be levelled in a more radical way. Suppose, for example, that a man acts in accordance with some virtue—say, helps a blind man across the road—but maintains that he has done so in order to develop his own benevolence. And in general let us imagine that this man does what he considers he ought, but does so in order to develop his own goodness. We should surely deny that this man was acting in a morally good way at all—his is rather a form of disguised egoism. Yet it might be argued that this man is satisfying the requirements of what we are calling private morality.

The objection is based on a conceptual confusion, a confusion which can be brought to light by considering two senses of 'good'.[16] In the first place, 'good' can mean 'that which is in a person's interests or will satisfy his desires'. It is this sense which is involved when we say, 'It is for your own good', and in this sense, 'my good' may conflict with 'your good'. In the second place, 'good' can be used to refer to whatever is thought to be worth pursuing or cherishing for its own sake, whatever is desirable as an end. It is in this sense that we might say (or presuppose, if we never actually *said* such a thing) that music is good or virtue good. Now if a person acts in accordance with a virtue, or otherwise acts in accordance with duty, but maintains that he is doing so 'for his own good', he might be misled into thinking he was so acting to develop his private morality. But in this he would be confused, for if he acted 'for his own good' he would be acting 'for his own interests', and his action would have no moral worth at all. But if he regards virtuous action as good in the second sense, then he is regarding it as worthwhile for its own sake, and the reference to 'his own' is inept. Hence, in so far as private morality requires a man to develop himself with respect to virtue, and in so far as virtue, to be counted as *moral* virtue, must be regarded as worth pursuing for its own sake, private morality must be distinguished from egoism. Similarly, in so far as the development of one's gifts is regarded as a duty of private morality (as distinct from a matter of inclination or interest) the gifts must be regarded as leading to activities good in themselves, and such development does not have an egoistic basis.

Now it may be contended that this argument, if it has proved anything, has proved rather too much. For, in so far as it makes clear that private morality requires us to develop our virtues and talents not as part of *our* good but as part of *the* good, it has ruled out the very possibility of a *private* morality at all. In reply it can be said that the sense of 'private' in which (we claim) there can be a private morality simply indicates the location in which a set of attributes can be developed—in the agent himself. And since it is in the agent himself that these characteristically human attributes can be developed or expressed he himself will have a peculiar responsibility for developing them. The fact that some of these attributes, particularly the virtues, can be developed only in acting for others in no way shows that their full significance as moral virtues is to be explained by their being dispositions exercised in the service of others. In serving others a person is also displaying distinctive human qualities and is thereby satisfying the demands of private morality. Again, in developing his natural talents a person is likewise acting *as* a person and thereby fulfilling the requirements of private morality.

9. SELF-RESPECT AND RESPECT FOR HUMAN NATURE

We have characterized social morality in terms of the principle of respect for persons, and it seems natural to assume that the concept which will enable us to link social and private morality is that of self-respect:[17] if respect for others is the supreme principle of public morality then respect for self is the supreme principle of private morality. And the *prima facie* justification for this assumption is greater than that of linguistic similarity, for we can say of a person, 'He has no self-respect', and mean that his conduct is morally deficient, that it is deficient in ways closely similar to ways in which he could fail to show respect for others, and that it essentially affects no one other than himself. But if these conditions can be satisfied it would seem that we can describe private morality, in the sense in which we are using the words 'private' and 'morality', in terms of self-respect. For example, if a man voluntarily allows himself to be systematically 'pushed around' by another person we might regard his undue submissiveness as a moral deficiency—a failure to respect in himself the ability to be self-determining, which is an essential aspect of being a person—and yet his conduct might not essentially affect anyone other than himself. We might say that the 'self' in 'self-respect' is basically the generic human self, and that we ought to respect human nature whether in our own person or in that of another. In this claim we should have the backing of Kant.

Unfortunately, there are good reasons for doubting that the private aspect of morality can be adequately analysed in terms of the *ordinary* concept of self-respect, and that 'self-respect' provides a link with respect for others. Doubt over the validity of a close comparison is suggested by the fact that whereas it is always a good thing to respect others, it does not always seem to be a good thing to respect oneself. For example, if a man says, 'I could never respect myself again if I did X', and then he does X, we think he ought to lose his self-respect. Thus, whereas it is sometimes morally appropriate that a man should lose self-respect, it is never morally appropriate that he should lose respect for others. This apparent counter-example should cause us to examine the argument which sought to establish a symmetry between respect for others and self-respect.

The argument that self-respect is for private morality what respect for others is for public morality depends on two premises: that if we take respect for others to be equivalent to respect for other selves, the sense of 'self' in both cases is the same, that is, that it is the generic human self or human nature, and not the idiosyncratic self of a specific person; and that the sense of 'respect' is the same in both cases. To cast doubt on one premise will be to cast doubt on the other at the same time, for, as we have argued in Chapter I, Section 3, there is a necessary connexion between the attitude of respect (or any other attitude) and its object. But the example of the previous paragraph, as well as showing that self-respect is not always a good thing, seems also to suggest that the senses of 'self' and of 'respect' are not the same in 'self-respect' as they are in 'respect for other (selves)'.

Consider first the sense of 'respect'. When a man says, 'I could never respect myself again if I did X', and then he does X, what he loses is his good opinion of himself. This suggests that the 'respect' in 'self-respect' is a favourable attitude towards oneself, whereas we have argued that 'respect' in 'respect for persons' is an attitude of *agape*. Indeed, it might be held that the sense of 'respect for others' which is analogous to self-respect is that involved when we admire someone for his talents or other good qualities. We say 'I respect his impartiality', and in a similar sense of 'respect', it may be argued, we respect ourselves when we have grounds for this attitude in our own qualities of character.

Now there is some truth in this analogy; it is at any rate nearer the truth than the analogy between the ordinary concept of self-respect and respect for persons. Nevertheless, it cannot be accepted as it stands, for respect for someone else, in the sense of thinking highly of him, implies that he is above the ordinary, has unusual merits. But *self*-respect does not imply this. A man who has self-respect merely thinks he comes up to scratch. Consider, for example, loss of self-respect. This does not merely mean ceasing to think well of oneself, but rather thinking badly of oneself, regarding oneself as inadequate, below par, and so on. The emotional aspect of loss of self-respect is not merely absence of pride or of pleasure in one's achievements, but disgust, contempt or despair. Self-respect then seems to be a man's attitude towards himself when he believes that he attains at least some minimum standard, and the emotion which goes with this, if any, is something like peace of mind. Loss of self-respect is the loss of this belief, either as a result of conduct judged to fall short of the minimum standard, or because for some reason a man comes to see himself in a new and unfavourable light. There is not, therefore, a *precise* parallel between self-respect in this sense and respect in the sense of admiration for the merits of others, but there is a similarity in that the object of the respect in both cases is an achievement—in the one case a positive achievement and in the other the modest achievement of living up to a minimum standard. These two senses of 'respect' are therefore more closely similar to each other than either is to the respect of 'respect for persons'.

But if the object of self-respect is an achievement, it follows that the sense of 'self' in 'self-respect' is the idiosyncratic rather than the generic sense. For an achievement is something which *distinguishes* a man from his fellows, or some of them, and not an attribute he shares with them. To respect one's own achievements is to respect something which is particular to oneself. So far then it seems that self-respect cannot correspond with respect for others.

It would be premature, however, to conclude from this that the concept of self-respect cannot aid us in linking public and private morality in terms of 'respect for persons', for the account of self-respect so far provided is lop-sided; it deals with only part of the concept, and possibly the less important part. This can be seen if we take into consideration the fact that self-respect can be an explanation of how a man behaves. As instances of this, consider expressions like 'Self-respect made me . . .' or 'Self-respect prevented me . . .' or again 'He did it out of self-respect'. Or again, we say to someone behaving badly, 'Have you no self-respect?', as if to imply that if he had, it would prevent him from behaving in this way. Now the idea of self-respect as a kind of not unfavourable opinion of oneself does not square very well with these usages. For one thing the self-respect which we have described earlier is something which is lost as a result of failure; but the usages above suggest that failure shows it to be absent already. Again, if we say to someone 'Have you no self-respect?' we suggest that self-respect is something which (like respect for others) everyone ought always to have; whereas it seems quite appropriate that someone who says 'I could never respect myself again if I did that' and then does it, should suffer a loss of self-respect. Most importantly, it is not clear how self-respect, construed as a belief in one's own adequacy, can explain acting or forbearing to act. It is not clear how a belief that one is already in some way satisfactory can be invoked as an explanation of satisfactory behaviour.

It seems that we have here what amounts to a second sense of the phrase 'self-respect'. Here it seems to stand for a motive, either a transient desire or one forming the basis of a permanent disposition. Usages such as 'out of self-respect' and 'self-respect made me' might refer either to passing desire or permanent disposition. Compare 'out of vanity' or 'jealousy made me'. Usages such as 'He refused because he has some self-respect' suggest a permanent disposition. Let us refer to this aspect of self-respect as the *conative* aspect, to distinguish it from the earlier sense, the 'favourable opinion' sense, which we may call the *estimative* aspect. These two aspects are closely linked in practice, but it is not at first sight obvious how they are linked. We shall try to show how they are linked presently, but shall first say a little more about the question hitherto slid over—that of the nature and source of the self-respect

standard. This is most easily investigated from the point of view of
conative self-respect—by considering, for example, what kinds of
shortcoming would provoke us to say: 'Have you no self-respect?'

First of all, a man is accused of lack of self-respect if he is willing
not to be his own master. A man who allows others to 'push him
around', who refuses to stand up for himself, who lets himself
be dependent or dominated, is naturally regarded as despicable,
to be looked down upon. He can also be looked upon as less than
human, in the sense that a human being (as we have argued in
Chapter I, Section 4) is characteristically self-determining; Sartre
would say that a man who refuses to acknowledge his ability to be
self-determining is behaving like a thing.

Whereas the attempt to be in some degree independent of others
is an essential part of self-respect, opinions will differ as to the
degree to which this is necessary if we are to say that someone has
self-respect, and also as to the way in which independence is really
manifested. For example, if someone is pushed about by an
officious administrator, it is not obvious whether self-respect
demands the making of a scene—'Nobody's going to treat *me* like
that'—or the *refusal* to be ruffled and 'put out', to allow him to
matter to that degree. Again, opinions would differ as to whether
a man who chooses for some definite idealistic reasons to submit to
others is lacking in self-respect—for example, a monk.

It should be noted that it is not the ability to get what one wants
which is demanded by self-respect. Very often a man's best method
of getting what he wants is to remain dependent on a benefactor—
for example, an indulgent parent—who will give him what he
wants. But such a man shows lack of self-respect because he is
allowing himself to be *passive*, not in control of the situation.
We may say: self-respect demands not only the fulfilment of one's
purposes, but the exercise of one's purposiveness. A man with self-
respect, then, will have the quality of independence; he will also
have tenacity, the refusal to be overcome by adverse circumstances.

Secondly, we accuse people of lack of self-respect if they are not
'their own masters' in a metaphorical sense—not in control of
themselves. We naturally identify the self with the reason and speak
of a man as 'not his own master' if reason is not in control: reasoned
behaviour is characteristic of mankind and so behaviour which is
unreasoned is thought of as subhuman. Thus we think of a man
who is 'enslaved' to drink, or who is swayed from his purposes by

emotion, as lacking in self-respect. It seems, then, that self-respect demands those virtues which are pre-eminently forms of self-control, such as courage and temperance.

So far, the standard with which conative self-respect is associated is partly objective and partly subjective. When we say that some-one has self-respect, we are attributing to him qualities of independence, tenacity and self-control. A man cannot have conative self-respect if he does not have these; whether he himself values them or not is immaterial. But within this objective framework there is room for subjective standards to play a large part. If a man is to be master of himself and his situation, this will involve meeting standards, attaining goals, fulfilling roles which he has set for *himself*. On the other hand again, the *fulfilment* of some roles is to be tested by an objective standard, even if the choice of role is a personal one.

This interaction of objective and subjective standards can be seen by examining the idiom 'No self-respecting x would. . .'. The 'x' here stands for the name of a role which has either been chosen or has at least been accepted and 'identified with', so that self-respect, which as we have seen requires the fulfilment of purposes, demands the performance of the role up to some minimum standard. What this standard is will largely be an objective matter. Thus a tutor may say to a student 'No self-respecting student would hand in work like this'. This suggests both that the work is bad by objective standards for students' work, and that it would not be so bad if the student had any self-respect as far as his role of student is concerned. Such a person takes no pride in his work, does not make good performance in it a point of honour. And because a person is normally thought to be responsible for having most of the roles he does have, we think of such a person as lacking self-respect in general. Thus if the student in the above example says, 'Well, I never wanted to be a student—people pushed me into it', the tutor might well reply, 'No self-respecting boy would allow such a thing to happen'.

Of course, there are some roles, such as those of sex, which we cannot be said to choose. Here there can be debate as to whether there is a role at all. Thus a statement like 'No self-respecting male would be seen pushing a pram' can be challenged either by questioning the appropriateness of this rule for male behaviour, or by questioning the assumption that there is a special role for men.

But it does not seem possible for a male accused of lack of self-respect to rebut the charge by saying 'I didn't choose to be a male' —any more than one can say 'I didn't choose to be a human being' when accused of subhuman behaviour. Self-respect demands the adequate enactment of some basic roles, which we find ourselves in rather than choose. This role-fulfilment then is a separate item in the list of types of behaviour demanded by self-respect and cannot entirely be subsumed under 'fulfilment of one's own purposes'.

The same can be said of the standards demanded by advantages and privileges which some have and not others. One might say for example: 'No self-respecting boy of any intelligence would read that'. Again, there is no rebuttal by saying 'I didn't choose to be intelligent'. An intelligent person is saddled with standards which do not apply to everyone but which he cannot fall below without degradation, whether or not *he* values his intelligence.

It has been suggested that some roles impose standards on us because we adopt them, others because we find ourselves in them. Some roles are a mixture of both: for example, the role of a gentleman. This can be looked on both as a code to which the individual chooses to commit himself—'Do you *call* yourself a gentleman?'— and also as a position of privilege, like the possession of intelligence, in which a man finds himself.

Now whatever is to be said about the detailed analysis of conative self-respect it is clear that the concept has close connexions with the features which were thought to be the distinctive endowment of a person—the abilities to be self-determining and rule-following. It might therefore seem reasonable to argue that, while estimative self-respect did not provide us with a link between public and private morality, conative self-respect does. Just as 'respect for persons' characterizes the motivation of the morally best other-regarding conduct, so, it can be maintained, 'conative self-respect' suggests the motivation of the morally best self-regarding conduct; and hence we have a conceptual bridge between the two aspects of morality.

But there are difficulties about accepting this conclusion. One difficulty is that the features of human nature with which conative self-respect is concerned are not invariably the 'generic' features we respect in other persons. As well as the abilities to be self-determining and rule-following, which set the basic standards for conative self-respect, there are also, as we have seen, the features which are peculiar to certain groups and which therefore set special standards for self-respect—features such as intelligence, sex, unchosen positions of privilege. But even if we concentrated on the generic features of human nature with which in any case conative self-respect is chiefly concerned, it is not clear that the motivation which conative self-respect provides us with is of the same kind as that provided in the attitude of respect for others.

One factor which may lead us to doubt the similarity in motivation is provided by the fact that an appeal to a man's conative self-respect may be used when an appeal to other morally good motives has failed. For example, suppose a man lives by sponging off his friends, deceiving them about his intentions of earning a wage of his own, making undue use of unemployment benefits, and so on. We might make a moral appeal to such a man by saying, 'Don't you think it wrong to treat your friends like that?', or, 'Don't you think it unfair to accept unemployment benefit when you could be earning a wage?', or, 'Don't you think it dishonest to accept loans which you have no intention of paying back?' Such appeals are clearly to the man's moral nature. But if they fail we might try asking 'Don't you even have any self-respect?', and in asking this we seem to be making an appeal to motivation of a different order from that of the moral appeals. We seem to be inviting the man to see his conduct as in some way beneath him; we are appealing to his concern that he should not be dishonoured, to his proper self-love (in Aristotle's sense).[18] This suggests that what we are appealing to is not the morally best motive (and therefore not the 'respect' of 'respect for persons') but rather one which is egoistically-tinged. Certainly it is a quality which is at least very useful in the moral life, providing very powerful incentives to virtue. An appeal to it is a good piece of moral strategy which can be applied to others or to oneself, but it seems too egoistic to be a proper basis for other-regarding conduct. If A is treated rightly by B 'out of self-respect' A may feel thankful that this safety net worked on B *faute de mieux*, but may also feel (appropriately, if our analysis of morality is on the right lines) that B, in treating him well for this reason alone, shows a lack of respect for others. And in a similar way, if A exercises his characteristic human qualities out of self-respect, then we may be glad that he does so at all, but we cannot regard his motivation as morally good.

It may be objected here that all we have shown is that where the good of *others* is concerned self-respect is too egoistic a motive. Certainly, the objector may say, we should respect others for their own sakes and not as a way of respecting ourselves. But it does not follow from this that self-respect is always too egoistic. If others are not concerned, as in many situations where self-respect is called for, what *is* the correct motive by contrast with which self-respect is found wanting? The answer to this objection will become clearer at the end of this section. For the present, we should note that, even within the sphere of actions which concern only oneself, it seems possible to draw a distinction between a man's concern that he should not be *dishonoured* (with stress on the standard) and his concern that *he* should not be dishonoured (with stress on himself). This distinction is not exactly the same as that between the generic and idiosyncratic selves, since both concerns equally may attach themselves to what befits a man as such. Rather it is between two qualities of motivation—self-regarding and self-forgetful.

We are now in a position to sum up the deficiencies of self-respect as a link between public and private morality. The concept has two aspects, which we called the estimative and the conative aspects. Estimative self-respect was deficient for our purposes in that the sense of 'self' involved was that of the 'idiosyncratic' self of the specific individual rather than that of the 'generic' self constituted by the distinctive human endowment; and consequently the sense of 'respect' was the 'not unfavourable opinion' sense rather than the '*agape*' sense. Conative self-respect involved the appropriate sense of 'self', but it was unsuitable for our purpose in that it suggested motivation of an egoistic type, which is not that of *agape*. Hence, self-respect, as that concept is used in ordinary discourse, cannot serve as the conceptual bridge to link private and public morality.

But if self-respect cannot provide a bridge it is not clear that we shall find a concept that will fare any better for this purpose. This should lead us to consider whether in fact we need a bridge at all. The argument that we do depends on the premise that public and private morality are two 'moralities', and that a link between them is consequently needed. But the discussion at the end of Section 8 of this chapter should lead us to question this premise. At the end of Section 8 we considered the objection that if we are required to develop our virtues or our gifts not as part of *our* good but as part of *the* good we will have ruled out the possibility of a *private* morality at all. Our reply was that the sense of 'private' in question simply indicates the location in which a set of attributes can be developed—in the agent himself. And since it is in the agent himself that these characteristically human attributes can be developed or expressed we argued that the agent himself has a peculiar responsibility for developing them. To say this, however, is to say that the agent has a duty to respect human nature in his own person. If, however, we say that respect for human nature in one's own person is the basis of private morality we can certainly link private and public morality, for they will appear not as two moralities but as two aspects of a single moral outlook characterized by the principle of respect for human nature in one's own person or in that of another. Social morality had as its supreme regulative principle that persons ought to be respected as ends, and to respect a person as an end meant to treat with sympathy his generic 'self' or his distinctive human endowment as a rule-following, self-determining being. But private morality depends on the same regulative principle, the relevant difference being that the agent himself is best placed to develop his own nature in certain ways. Thus the fundamental moral principle governing private morality is the same as that governing public or social morality—respect for human nature, whether in one's own person or in that of another.

10. CONCLUSION

In this chapter we argued that there is an aspect of morality which can be called 'private' in that it concerns the agent's conduct *vis-à-vis* himself. The presence of this aspect of morality is reflected in the judgements of praise and blame we make about the virtues; our praise of the courageous man (for example) is not entirely to be analysed in terms of his utility. Again, the private side to morality may be involved when we judge that a man ought to develop his distinctive endowment as a human being irrespective of its possible utility. Indeed, the obligation to develop one's gifts may sometimes successfully compete with some duties of social morality, and, since only a duty can override a duty, it seems clear that what we have called 'private morality' is no less basic than its public counterpart. It is important, however, to distinguish private morality from what is ordinarily meant by 'self-respect'; self-respect in its estimative form involves the wrong senses of 'self' and 'respect' and in its conative form is too egoistic a concept to provide a link with the principle of respect for persons. Nevertheless, we can say that private morality is concerned with respecting the distinctive human endowment as we find it in ourselves, whereas public morality is concerned with respecting the distinctive human endowment as we find it in others; private and public morality are therefore not two moralities, but two aspects of a single fundamental moral principle.

CHAPTER IV

RESPECT FOR PERSONS
AND MORAL RESPONSIBILITY

I. RESPECT, RESPONSIBILITY AND PURPOSE

WE argued in Chapter I that a person as a rational will is essentially a self-determining, rule-following creature, and that to respect him as such is to make his ends one's own and to take into account that he can govern his conduct by rules. But to regard a person in this way is to take seriously his conduct and to assume that as a rational agent he does in fact intend to do what he does and that his conduct is to be explained in terms of his stated or inferred aims. This is to say that it is to be explained in purposive language, by which we mean expressions of the form 'He did A in order to get B', or 'He did X because he wanted Y'.

There is a feature of such explanations which is often overlooked but is nevertheless of the first importance; they presuppose a choice or decision to let the desire for the end carry us into action.* This is brought out by the fact that to an explanation of the form 'I did A because I wanted B' it is always possible to add 'and I *chose* to act on my desire'. Moreover, this addition is required for logical completeness (although, of course, it is often considered redundant within the context of ordinary discourse). For people very often have desires on which they do not act. Thus in a detective story several people may have motives for the crime, that is, they have aims in terms of which the committing of the crime might be explained; but only one of the suspects acts on his desire. There is therefore a gap between desire and action, and it is possible to say that the concept of choice or decision fills it.

Now it is because the actions of persons can be explained purposively that we attribute responsibility to persons—hold, that is,

* It should be noted that we are concerned with purposive explanation of human action; we do not consider the meaning of purposive explanation when it is extended to sub-human behaviour.

that the actions of persons are *theirs* in a sense which makes it appropriate to praise or blame them for performing such actions. This can be seen by considering the circumstances in which we withdraw our assumption that a person is responsible for what he does. For it emerges that these circumstances are identical with those which would lead us to regard explanations of actions in purposive terms as inappropriate. The circumstances—'excusing conditions' as they are often called—are roughly those in which it can be shown that the agent was in some sense compelled to act as he did or in which he did not really know what he did. For example, we do not hold a person morally responsible for knocking an old lady off the pavement if he was himself pushed; and clearly this is a case in which purposive explanations do not apply. Again, if a person has acted in ignorance of the facts he is not held morally responsible for the action which was done in ignorance; and clearly an action cannot be explained purposively under any description which the agent does not know to apply.

In our sketch of excusing conditions we have taken no account of complexities, but perhaps we have said enough to establish that purposiveness is the condition for responsibility to which the excusing conditions point. In other words, pleas of compulsion or ignorance excuse because they indicate that purposive explanations are not applicable in the usual manner, that since the agent was acting in ignorance or under compulsion he did not choose to do what he did. In normal cases, however, purposiveness and thus responsibility are assumed. We shall later need to investigate more precisely what is involved in purposive explanation if it is to justify the ascription of moral responsibility. For the present, however, we can simply note that if a person is to be held responsible for an action it must be possible to explain the action in terms like 'He did A because he desired B (and he chose to act on his desire)'.

2. DETERMINISM

We have argued that purposive language is an indispensable part of the discourse we use in describing and explaining our actions at an everyday level. Before we can decide on the significance to attach to this mode of discourse we must take into account rather different considerations. These may be described, grandly, as the considerations which make science a rational pursuit, or, more humbly, as the considerations which enable us to make sense of the events in our everyday life. They are, in short, the assumptions implicit in the spectator attitude to the world. We all can and do regard the world not only as agents with intentions but also as spectators of its events. Now essential to the spectator attitude to the world is the principle that every event has a cause. It is essential in so far as it is not possible to make sense of the interactions of things in the world without assuming the principle, for to 'make sense' of the world of things and events is in fact to find causal explanations, which assume the existence of causal laws. It may be objected that science no longer accepts the universal validity of the principle of causality, on the grounds that a branch of science— quantum mechanics—proceeds without assuming the principle, and indeed suggests that the principle does not hold of the sub-microscopic world it investigates. The laws of quantum mechanics, it may be said, are not causal but statistical. However that may be, we have been given no reason to suppose that the principle of causality does not govern the macroscopic world of the senses, and it is with the world of the large-scale that the majority of the special sciences are concerned. Let us assume, then, that the principle of causality governs the scientific investigation of the large-scale world as well as our ordinary spectator outlook on it. What bearing does this assumption have on our interpretation of purposive language and consequently of moral responsibility?

The answer to this question emerges in outline if to the thesis that every event has a cause we add another—that human actions are like events in many respects. This may lead us to consider plausible the hypothesis that human actions have causes. Now if we interpret a 'cause'—as it is natural to do at a common sense level—as 'that which makes an event happen', we seem forced to conclude that our actions are 'made to happen'. But, as we have seen in our account of excusing conditions, if actions are made to happen we do not feel justified in using purposive types of explanation, and as a result doubt our responsibility for them. Hence, starting from the spectator view-point of the world and proceeding by steps which seem easy to take, we have finished with a conclusion which suggests that responsibility is an illusion and purposive explanation no more than a linguistic convenience. To accept the validity of such a pattern of argument is to accept the challenge of determinism.

3. THE REDUCIBILITY THESIS

According to some interpretations of its general thesis, however, the challenge of determinism may be met without damage to our ordinary assumptions about persons and their actions. Such interpretations attempt to show that our ordinary assumptions about action and responsibility are quite compatible with determinism because purposive language can be *reduced* to causal language. Consider, for example, the specific theory we shall call 'psychological determinism'.

The psychological determinist agrees that we may legitimately use purposive language in explaining actions and that we rightly assume ourselves to be morally responsible for our actions. He also agrees that actions are events and as such are open to sufficient explanation in causal terms. His solution of this apparent antinomy is to suggest, firstly, that it is at best misleading to say that the causes of human action *compel* (since they are the agent's own choices), but it may even be actually false to regard any causes as compelling events to happen; secondly, that purposive types of explanation (including the 'choice' requirement) are all reducible to explanations in terms of desire; and thirdly, that desires are causes (but only in the non-coercive, 'innocent' manner to be made clear in the development of the first step). The aim of this argument is to reduce purposive explanation to causal and so preserve both the agent's assumption of moral responsibility and the spectator's assumption of causation. Let us examine the steps of the argument.

The first step is to point out that, on our analysis, that which gives rise to action is the agent's own choice, and it is misleading to regard this as something which 'compels' an action to happen. 'Compulsion', it may be said, simply means 'absence of choice'. Hence, if the psychological determinist is correct in interpreting choice as a cause it is not fair to say he is suggesting that we are acting under compulsion. Moreover, the psychological determinist usually endorses the empiricist analysis of causation. If so, he will deny that it is meaningful to speak in general of causes as 'compelling'. On the empiricist analysis, causal laws simply record regular conjunctions of events, what in fact happens in nature, and do not require us to speak of compulsion.[1] Since we wish to avoid extended discussion on the nature of causation we shall simply

G

concede to the psychological determinist the first step in his argument.

His second step is to assert that purposive explanations are all reducible to explanations in terms of the agent's desires. Now it is true that we have already defined purposive statements (verbally at least) as those which can be cast in the form 'I did A because I wanted B', but we stressed that the desire for the end presupposed in purposive explanations is never a sufficient condition of action, for it is always possible (and required for logical completeness) to add 'and I chose to act on my desire for B'. It follows, then, that if the psychological determinist is to make out a case for reducing purposive explanations to causal he must be able to reduce choice to desire. The case is characteristically made out by the drawing of a distinction between the mere occurrence of 'blind' desire and the modification such desire may receive after the agent has deliberated about the consequences of acting upon it and other desires he may have. Ross, for example, regards choice as the expression of the strongest desire at the moment of action, while desire is for him the joint product of the antecedent states of character and beliefs about the circumstances.[2] Desire need not be either 'blind' or 'compulsive', however, for although each single desire may be concentrated on a single feature of an imagined future it is possible to deliberate about the consequences of following one desire or another and thus strengthen some desires and weaken others. For Ross, then, choice is the result of this reflective survey of our desires and their believed consequences; it is simply 'processed' desire. Let us, for the moment at least, concede this second step in the reducibility thesis of psychological determinism.

The third step consists of the claim that desire is a cause. Is this plausible? One criticism of the claim might be that desires are in the wrong category to be causes, for whereas desires are states a cause must be an event. The psychological determinist might concede this claim (though a case could be made out against it) but he would go on to point out, as we have seen, that the cause of action is not desire *simpliciter* but the processed desire which he calls choice and which can be seen as an event.

A second criticism might be that whereas a cause is externally or contingently connected with its effect a desire is internally or necessarily connected with action.[3] The argument from the internal relation of desire and action has in fact two sides to it which may easily be confused. The first is that a desire must be internally related to the action said to be done 'because he wanted to do it', in that the desire cannot be identified other than as a desire to perform such and such an action. For example, if I have a desire to write to Aunt Maud I can identify the desire only by saying that it is a desire to write to Aunt Maud. The second side to the argument is that an action X which is explained purposively by reference to a desire Y logically must be describable in terms of Y. For example, if someone says 'Why are you buying an airmail form?' and I reply 'Because I want to write to Aunt Maud' then my action, 'buying an airmail form', must be describable as 'a step towards writing to Aunt Maud', 'a means of writing to Aunt Maud' or the like. If it is not so describable then it does not provide a purposive explanation. Desire and action must therefore be regarded as internally related in that a desire to act cannot logically be identified except as a desire for a certain specified action, and an action X which is purposively explained in terms of a desire Y must logically be describable in terms of the desire. On the other hand, most psychological determinists endorse the empiricist analysis of causation whereby a cause and its effect are conjoined by simple contingency.

In reply it can be said that whereas it is *things* or *events* which are causally related it is *descriptions* of things or events which are internally related. Thus the fact that a desire to act can be identified in description only in terms of the desired action does not show that it is impossible for there to be a causal relation between the occurrence of the desire and the occurrence of the desired action. For example, even though my desire to write to Aunt Maud can be *described* only as a desire to write to Aunt Maud, it can still be the case that the occurrence of that desire (of which I can be aware quite independently of the occurrence of the action) may cause me to write to Aunt Maud.

And *a fortiori* (to reply to the second side of the argument), the fact that the action to be explained purposively must be describable in a way which mentions the explanatory desire goes no way towards showing that the occurrence of the desire and the occurrence of the action cannot be causally related. For in this case the desire and the action, although they must be describable in terms of each other, *can* also be described in quite separate ways, as for example 'the desire to write to Aunt Maud' and 'buying an airmail form'. In any case, we can equally give a description of a *cause* in terms of its effect, and *vice versa*. Thus, the fact that we can describe lung cancer as 'an effect of smoking' does not show that smoking cannot cause lung cancer. Similarly (the psychological determinist may argue), the fact that we can describe buying an airmail form as 'taking steps towards writing to Aunt Maud' does not show that the desire to write to Aunt Maud cannot cause a man to buy an airmail form. In other words, the psychological determinist might simply construe expressions like 'means to X' or 'steps to X' as equivalent to 'actions caused by a desire for X' or, more accurately, 'actions caused by a desire for X combined with the belief that they will further the attainment of X'. The argument from internal relations, in either aspect, does not then constitute an unanswerable objection to the psychological determinist.

A third criticism of the claim that a desire can be a cause might be based on a behavioural analysis of desire (such as that provided by Professor G. Ryle).[4] In terms of this analysis it might be said that desire is to be defined in terms of the phenomena which are normally said to be done 'because he wanted X'. The analogy to which it is helpful to appeal in expounding this view is that of the syndrome and the symptoms which make it up. Thus, philosophers say that part of what we *mean* by desiring a thing is that the desirer should try to get it. On such a view, then, it would not make sense to say that a desire caused its characteristic actions, since the occurrence of the desire is not an item separable from the occurrence of the actions in question. Hence, if the psychological determinist adopts a behavioural account of desire he cannot (while remaining a *psychological* determinist) regard a desire as a cause, for on this analysis the phrase 'because he wanted to do X' does not provide a causal explanation but rather an invitation to see the action in a certain light, as part of a pattern of actions, thoughts, feelings etc. with a certain structure.

Now the force of this argument obviously depends on the validity of a behavioural analysis of desire, and such an analysis may well be criticized. Consider, for example, the agent's privileged knowledge of his own desires. On the Rylean analysis a man's knowledge of his own desires is in principle the same as his knowledge of other people's desires; he finds out by observing what he does. But while we may admit that occasionally a man discovers that he wants something by observation of this kind, the normal situation seems to be that a man possesses an awareness of his own desires which is not derived from observation.[5] It may well be, as we have already allowed, that a desire cannot logically be *described* without reference to the desired actions, but it does not follow from this that desires are not identifiable by the agent independently of the *occurrence* of the desired action; the agent can know what he desires without waiting to see what he does. Hence, if desire can occur independently of action there is no logical reason why it cannot count as a cause of action. Moreover, as we have seen in the argument of the second step, it can be maintained that choice, the sufficient condition of action, is analysable in terms of desire (understood as 'processed' by rational deliberation). We have therefore completed the case for a causal reduction of purposive explanation, in so far as this can be done by psychological determinism.

The question now arises whether explanations of actions, in terms of a choice analysable in this (causal) manner, leave room for moral responsibility. To give an adequate answer to this question we would need to take up again the issue shelved at the end of Section 1—that of what is required of purposive explanation if it is to justify the ascription of responsibility. And we shall take this issue up again, but not till we have discussed the compatibility thesis of physical determinism in our next section. In the meantime we shall reject the reducibility thesis of psychological determinism on quite different grounds—on the grounds that it does not do justice to the *epistemology* of decision and action from the agent's point of view, and thus to the logic of action-descriptions.

To see the force of the epistemological argument, consider the nature of the agent's knowledge of his own future actions. For the psychological determinist, who sees actions as caused by choices expressing the strongest desire, such knowledge (where it exists) must be *inductive*, for it is on the basis of induction that we predict causally governed events. But it may be argued, as it has been by Professor Stuart Hampshire,[6] that a man can have privileged knowledge of his own future actions which would not be possible on the basis of induction. It may well be true that a man can use his inductive knowledge of himself in order to say, 'Experience teaches me that in a certain situation I shall *desire* to do X'. But this statement is in a different logical category from a statement of intention. A man's privileged knowledge of what he is going to do is based not on inductive knowledge of the alleged causes of action, but rather on his own *decisions* to act in a certain way.

It may be further argued by the advocates of the Hampshire position that the agent's privileged knowledge of his own future actions raises difficulties for the whole programme of psychological determinism. To see why this non-predictive knowledge has been thought to be a threat to determinism, consider why it is thought that an agent's knowledge of his own future actions must be 'decisive' rather than predictive. The reason is that no prediction of his own actions with which an agent is presented can ever be final, whether he arrives at it himself or is informed of someone else's prediction. He can always 'step back' from it and make a *decision*, either to let events take their course or to endeavour to falsify the prediction. Since he will usually succeed in falsifying such a prediction if he tries (the anti-determinist will say) this ability to stand back and decide constitutes freedom; and a man who regards his own actions as predictable is trying to avoid the responsibility of this freedom by pretending to himself that no decisions are involved. If an agent says to himself, 'I know that when the time comes I'll do nothing, because I'm a coward', we can reply, 'Have you then *decided* to do nothing?'

It seems arguable, then, that without even raising the more fundamental question of whether a causal reduction of purposive explanation would enable us to do justice to the essential nature of choice and responsibility, we can reject the thesis of psychological determinism on epistemological grounds. Even if we allow that causes do not compel, and that desires are in the right logical category to be causes, we cannot conclude that actions are caused by desires. For our desires give rise to actions if, but only if, we decide or choose to let them; and the occurrence of choice or decision cannot be analysed causally in terms of *psychological* determinism. If it could, our knowledge of what we are going to do would be inductive or predictive. But it is not of this nature; our certainty that we are going to do A rather than B (unless we are prevented or change our mind) is rather to be classed as 'decisive' than as inductive or predictive. We therefore reject psychological determinism on epistemological grounds (leaving it for the moment open whether or not it can *also* be rejected on the grounds that its attempted causal reduction does not do justice to the essential nature of choice). With the rejection of the reducibility thesis goes the hope that the assumptions of the agent standpoint can be reconciled with those of the spectator by the *identification* of purposive types of explanation with one sort of causal explanation.

4. THE COMPATIBILITY THESIS

But this view of the agent's non-predictive knowledge of his own decisions or choices seems to secure only what we may call 'subjective freedom'—the logical necessity of the agent's regarding *himself* as free. The *physical* determinist may argue that the agent's decisions, including his decisions about predictions, are themselves predictable in principle on a basis of knowledge of physical causation; and thus that the agent is not the final authority on what he is going to do. And while it may be maintained that no one determinist on his own can predict everything (on the grounds that part of what is to be predicted will depend on his own decisions) this seems to be a limitation on science rather than a loophole for freedom—a fact of epistemology rather than of metaphysics. In other words, the physical determinist is conceding that we can legitimately use purposive language in our explanation of action—he is granting that the basic psychological concepts of action such as decision or choice are not causal—but he goes on to argue that decisions etc. have physical counterparts in the brain, and that he can provide a sufficient causal explanation of these necessary physical counterparts of decision.

It should be noted, however, that if the physical determinist is going to give 'teeth' to his thesis he must be precise in his interpretation of 'physical counterpart'. It can be agreed by all that decisions have physical correlates in the sense that unless certain physical conditions obtain—the person's brain is in good working order, various nervous impulses occur etc.—a decision causally cannot be made. To admit this is simply to admit that the occurrence of physical events is a necessary condition of the making of a decision. The physical determinist, however, must say more than this. He must maintain that decisions and the like have physical *determinants* in the brain, that the occurrence of physical events is both a necessary and a sufficient condition of the occurrence (for 'occurrence' it would really be) of a decision. If, but only if, he interprets 'physical counterpart' in this strong sense does the physical determinist raise serious difficulties for our position.

The thesis of the physical determinist can be made more drama-tically compelling if it is expressed in terms of an analogy between the human brain and nervous system and a computer. The argu-ments of the physical determinist are apt to seem unconvincing if they seem to be saying that the human brain is just a machine; for whereas the conception of a machine stimulated the imagination of writers in the seventeenth and early eighteenth centuries it now seems hopelessly inadequate as an analogy to explain the workings of the human brain. The conception of the computer, however, is to the imagination of the twentieth century what that of the machine was to earlier centuries—a model which, in its close parallels with the workings of the brain, helps us to understand what is otherwise mysterious. Now a computer, it can be argued, is a physically determined system: it is an input/output mechanism in which every event can be causally connected with sets of pre-ceding events. And so it is with the brain.

It should be noted that the position of the physical determinist on this matter is not open to the same objections which we raised over psychological determinism. As we have seen, the *psychological* determinist's causal analysis of the occurrence of decision implies that we can know by experience what we shall decide; and whereas it is intelligible to say that we know by experience what desires are likely to occur in a certain context, it does not seem intelligible to say that we similarly know by experience what decisions are likely to occur. The physical determinist, however, is not concerned with the epistemology of decision and action, nor therefore with the logic of our action-descriptions. He can concede that the *agent* does not know by induction how he is going to act, but he will maintain that the *scientific spectator* can (at least in principle) have inductive knowledge of the occurrence of the physical determinants of decision processes. The inductive knowledge relevant to physical determinism is the scientist's knowledge of brain-states alleged to be the determinants of what the agent may from his point of view call a 'decision'.

The question now arises whether physical determinism, so understood, can be reconciled with the assumptions of the agent standpoint. Can our ordinary concepts of responsibility or action survive the causal explanations which the physical determinist claims he can provide of the decisions which lead to action? If we recall that we originally saw responsibility as depending on the applicability of purposive explanation we can ask this question in another way, and consider whether purposive explanation of a type which would justify the ascription of responsibility can survive such explanations.

Now it is true that we have already shown purposive explanation in terms of choice or decision to be irreducible to causal explanation. But the physical determinist might well admit this. His thesis would then be that purposive explanation can never oust or show to be inapplicable a causal explanation in physical terms. This does not mean that he will dismiss purposive explanation as meaningless or as referring to some kind of illusion. On the contrary, many philosophers will say that causal and purposive modes of explanation are complementary and can exist quite satisfactorily side by side. In short, they maintain that even if purposive explanation is not *reducible* to causal explanation it is *compatible* with it.

In order to examine this thesis of compatibility we shall now need to take up the question which we shelved at the end of Section 1, and again when discussing psychological determinism— that of the nature of those purposive explanations on which responsibility rests. We earlier said that the 'excusing conditions' absolve a man from responsibility in that they show that purposive explanations do not apply, and we defined 'purposive explanation' very vaguely at that stage as explanation which logically could be put in the verbal form, 'I did A because I wanted B (and chose to act on my desire)'. But we shall now try to go beyond this account and consider what must be the nature of the purposiveness which lies behind the idea of responsibility.

In its fundamental nature this conception of purposiveness seems to involve, not simply choice, but an undetermined choice— a choice which could have been different in exactly the same situation. For if purposiveness is to be the criterion of responsible action, it must be taken to allow that the agent could have done otherwise than he did. This seems to be demanded by the notion that it is *his* action—that he is responsible for it, in the sense of making it what it is. We suggest, then, that those explanations of action which betoken responsibility, such as 'I did it because I wanted . . .', imply also 'I did it because I chose to do it'—construing choice in the sense above, which embodies the notion that in a particular set of circumstances a choice may go one way or the other. In other words, we maintain that responsibility entails the 'categorical substitutability'[7] of choices, i.e. the possibility that the choice might be different, not merely *if* the circumstances were also different, but different in the same circumstances. We can also say that responsibility entails the categorical substitutability of *actions*. This is not really a separate factor from the categorical substitutability of choices. Rather our view is that responsible action is action which embodies a choice of an undetermined kind; and to describe this situation we can speak indifferently of the categorical substitutability of actions or of the categorical substitutability of choices.

It might of course be said that 'I did it because I chose to' does not add anything to an explanation. After all, it does not necessarily even explain an action in terms of an antecedent, since choice of this kind need not precede the action but may be manifested in the actual performing of it. But the force of the explanation lies not in what it says but in what it excludes. For if such an explanation implies that the circumstances might all have been exactly the same but the choice or chosen action different, it rules out a causal explanation of the same action: in causal terms, only one effect can follow a given set of circumstances. We might strengthen our position by pointing out that if an action can be causally explained, it is fixed long before the person concerned is born (indeed, from the beginnings of the universe); and an action thus determined would not be the *agent's* action at all, for what happens entirely depends on factors completely beyond his control. The chosen action, on the other hand, is the agent's own doing; he may be circumscribed by features which he cannot influence, including his own desires, but some room is left for his own decision to contribute to events.

Now it may be objected here that this picture of the agent's situation rests on one particular view of causality—the view which goes beyond the empirical phenomena, and sees causality in terms of the influence or power one thing has over another. Our notion that the agent's action is 'fixed long before he is born' embodies this non-empirical view, as on the empirical view nothing can be said to influence what happens later; it just does happen. We can however avoid this objection by resting our case on the non-substitutability of what can be causally explained, a feature shared by both views of causality. But it may well be that an adequate account of responsibility entails a non-empiricist view of causality in the sphere of human action. For the notion that an action is an agent's *own* does suggest that he can control or at least influence what happens by what he does.

We can now see that the psychological determinist's account (which we rejected on merely epistemological grounds) is not in fact an account of *choice* at all—at least, not in any sense which could do justice to responsibility. For on that account the so-called choice is not something which the man himself makes—it is made for him. We have of course asserted this point before, at the level of the epistemology of the agent standpoint and the logic of the concepts applicable to it. But we can now see that the deficiency of psychological determinism is not merely that it cannot account for the epistemology and logic of choice, but that it cannot accommodate the essential nature of choice itself, as the basic factor of responsible action. We can also see that no form of causal explanation of action, if it is complete, can be compatible with this kind of purposive explanation. For the effect of a causal explanation would necessarily be to undercut the explanation in terms of choice, by suggesting that the outcome in the way of action did not turn on the agent's choice but was in any case settled; whereas the essence of responsibility is that explanation with reference to choice must be the final or ultimate explanation of why one action is performed rather than another, even if causality can contribute something to explanation in the form of a framework of circumstances.

To illustrate and generalize our claim that complete causal explanation is incompatible with purposive explanation (where that is adequate to the concept of responsibility) we shall consider two attempts by Professor P. F. Strawson to make out a case for the compatibility thesis, one in terms of complementary descriptions or modes of explanation and the other in terms of complementary attitudes.

Strawson's first argument is the following:[8] 'I agree that we might, for some purposes, describe a particular bit of human behaviour in terms of "moving parts". But I don't agree that such descriptions would be adequate to the concept of human action. . . . The first sort of descriptions might indeed all find a place in, or under, physical explanatory laws. . . . But the second and indispensable sort could find no such place. They belong to a different kind of vocabulary and call for a place in a wholly different dimension of explanation.' In a later passage he argues (as a philosophical, rather than as a scientific thesis) that 'there are no effective correlations between the two vocabularies for talking about what goes on, the vocabulary of human action and the vocabulary of physical science.' The conclusion, then, seems to be that human action cannot be fully explained in terms of physical events, but since physical determinism is concerned precisely with physical events it constitutes no threat to our ordinary concepts of action and responsibility. Strawson thus holds, in effect, that causal and purposive explanation are compatible because causal explanation is not really explanation of *action* at all, but only of moving parts, etc.

Before we can decide whether this reconciliation bid is acceptable, we must disentangle a confusion which arises out of the ambiguity of the language in which the argument is stated. The ambiguity is in the loose use of expressions such as 'explained in terms of', 'described in terms of' or 'different kinds of vocabulary'. It may well be the case that actions cannot be adequately *described in terms of* physical events, but this claim (which we can concede) is quite distinct from the claim that actions cannot be adequately *explained in terms of* physical events, if by 'explained in terms of' we mean 'causally accounted for by'. It is the second claim which is relevant to Strawson's attempt to reconcile causal and purposive explanation. For the first claim would be consistent with the thesis that actions had causes and that these were describable in physical terms even if the actions themselves were not so describable; whereas Strawson hopes to show that causal explanation cannot apply to action.

But even if we grant the second claim without argument, and assume that physical causes can have only physical effects, Strawson has not succeeded in preserving our ordinary concepts of action and responsibility. For it is clear that, although action-descriptions cannot be reduced to movement-descriptions, our actions cannot be free in the sense which responsibility requires if our movements are determined. There is certainly more to signing a cheque than the movements of my hand, but if my movements are determined then it is no longer an open possibility that I may either sign it or not sign it. I shall be causally determined to do either the one or the other. Strawson's first reconciliation bid, in terms of complementary vocabularies, descriptions or modes of explanation, seems therefore to be unsuccessful. For even if we allow that physical causes can produce only movements and that actions are not describable in terms of movements, the claim that movements are determined is incompatible with belief in responsible action.

Strawson's second attempt[9] at reconciliation is in terms of attitudes. Whereas in the first attempt the objects of the complementary explanations were presented as distinct, here the object of the complementary attitudes is the same—an action in both cases. The key distinction in the second attempt is that between a 'reactive' or 'participant' attitude and an 'objective' attitude. The reactive attitude (or range of attitudes) is that which characterizes the inter-personal behaviour of normal adults. The general nature of an 'objective' attitude emerges by contrast when, taking the special case of resentment, he considers the types of circumstance in which our reactive attitudes would or ought to be suspended. The first range of cases covers coercion or lack of knowledge: when these factors are operative we suspend our reactive attitude, not to the agent in general, but only to the particular action. In the second range of cases we do suspend our reactive attitude to the agent, either temporarily—as in cases of illness—or permanently—as in cases of insanity. The appropriate attitude in the second range of cases is 'objective' in Strawson's sense of the term; it is the appropriate attitude when there are (in our terminology) excusing conditions.

Now Strawson does not say what such factors have in common, other than a tendency to promote objective attitudes, but it is tempting to say that what promotes the objective attitudes is the belief that the operation of these factors renders the behaviour open to sufficient explanation in causal terms. And this temptation becomes the harder to resist when we consider that he tells us[10] that to adopt the objective attitude to a person is to see him as suitable for treatment or cure and as unsuitable for reasoning with; it is to view him as 'something to be understood and controlled in the most desirable fashion'.[11] It is hard to make sense of these passages unless we assume that to adopt the objective attitude to someone (Strawson's use of *something* in the last quotation may be significant) is to view his conduct as open to sufficient explanation and control in causal terms. Indeed, it is not clear that an attitude can be *identified* as objective in Strawson's sense unless we assume that it is that which fittingly arises with the awareness that behaviour can be sufficiently explained in causal terms.

Now, in so far as he has introduced the objective attitude as that which one ought to adopt towards abnormal behaviour, Strawson has remained on safe ground. But he goes on to suggest that it is possible in *normal* cases to inhibit the reactive attitude and adopt the objective. We can do this, he tells us,[12] to escape 'the strain of involvement; or as an aid to policy; or simply out of intellectual curiosity'. Yet, whatever the motives, the adoption of the objective attitude would again seem to be intelligible (or even identifiable) only if we assume that a sufficient explanation of normal behaviour can be provided in causal terms. But to assume the sufficiency of such terms is to cast doubt on the ultimacy of what the agent himself offers as his reasons or intentions. If this is so, the reactive attitude would appear to be in some sense less ultimate than the objective. Such a position is not likely to bring about a reconciliation, since it casts doubt on the whole conception of responsible action and the types of explanation appropriate to it.

A similar failure is to be expected if the compatibility thesis is asserted in any other way, whether in terms of complementary language games, universes of discourse, levels of analysis or types of explanation. It is true that in a minimal sense complete causal explanations and purposive explanations might be regarded as complementary. This sense could be illustrated by a puppet show in which a commentator gives significance to the movements of the puppets by his commentary. But such explanations or descriptions of the movements are not equal in status with, but, on the contrary, are undercut by the complete causal explanations which can be provided by an account of the jerkings of the wires behind the scenes. Or again, there is a sense in which a person who had been hypnotized might offer purposive explanation of what he was doing, but we know that the correct and sufficient explanation is to be found in the effects of the hypnotist's suggestions. Partnership on such terms is not acceptable.

5. PURPOSIVE EXPLANATION

The position is that to make sense of our ordinary conceptions of action we must maintain the ultimacy of the purposive mode of explanation, and to maintain the ultimacy of the purposive mode we must maintain the categorical substitutability of chosen actions. The consequence is that we cannot reconcile the standpoints of the agent and of the observer of events, and we must conclude that, if we are to hold on to our ordinary concepts of action, we must deny that actions are always open to sufficient explanation in causal terms.

How then are we to explain why people perform those actions which they do perform? Let us suppose that a person says, 'I did A because I chose to do it'. Clearly this does not amount to an explanation so much as a *claim*: 'I am responsible for this action' or 'This action is mine'. If such a claim is made we can go on to ask: 'Why did you choose to do it?' To this question a typical answer would be 'Because I wanted such-and-such', and this reply seems to explain the action in a way in which the bare mention of choice does not—it is informative. Therefore, in discussing purposive explanation of action, we must remember that such explanation has two components: a choice component which (as we have seen) serves merely negatively to exclude causal explanation, and a desire component, which provides positive information.

But what kind of information does such explanation provide? Needless to say, it does not provide causal explanation. Though our desires may be accountable for in terms of causes, they do not in turn cause our choices; this has been the whole burden of the previous section. But mention of a desire shows the point of a choice or makes sense of it. For example, if we ask why a man decided to tidy his garden and are told that he wants to sell his house, we see the point of his decision. The explanation sets the chosen action in a framework: sometimes, as here, a framework of familiar human purposes; sometimes a framework which may itself require illumination by reference to a further want. And this is the kind of explanation which we are ordinarily looking for when we ask why someone does something.

We maintain, then, that the only informative explanation of responsible action is of the 'because he wanted' type, to be construed not as giving a cause but as showing the point or sense of an action. Is this good enough? It certainly compares unfavourably with causal explanation. A complete causal explanation of an event makes it clear why the event occurred exactly when and how it did; we understand why it could not have been otherwise unless the circumstances had been other than they were. A purposive explanation (if it is to do what responsibility requires of it) logically cannot offer this precision. For such explanation must allow that any given rational choice could have been other than what it was without a change in circumstances, desires or the like. Another action could have been substituted; and this 'could' is the unqualified or categorical 'could' and not 'could *if* some condition had been different'. Now if the explanations of action required by responsibility are compatible with the categorical substitutability of other actions then they obviously compare unfavourably with those provided by the determinist. We are claiming that there is a breakdown of the possibility of causal explanation in the case of human action, and to make a claim of this nature is also to admit that, despite the possibility of explanations in purposive language, there are limitations to our understanding of rational action.

It may be objected here that what is missing from purposive explanations is simply *predictability*; that we cannot base the prediction of a future action on a purposive explanation as we can base the prediction of a future event on a complete causal explanation. Nevertheless, the argument may go on, *intelligibility* is provided by purposive explanations and that is all we require in our explanations of human action. This is the view put forward by Richard Taylor,[13] and in general we agree with it. But purposive explanation certainly has shortcomings—practical and theoretical—as compared with complete causal explanation. We shall mention two of them.

To begin with the practical shortcoming, we would sometimes like to predict human behaviour, not just to a degree of probability, but with certainty, as when we are appointing someone to a post which will put great pressures on him. But predictions of this kind are not even in principle possible on the basis of purposive explanation. Secondly, it must be admitted that even if a purposive explanation makes an action fully intelligible to the person asking about it, it is an odd sort of intelligibility which is compatible with the action's either having been performed or not performed. Yet we must insist on the latter condition's being satisfied if we are to have explanations of action which are compatible with the assumption of moral responsibility. It would seem, then, that although purposive explanation does in general make rational action intelligible, it is in some ways less satisfactory than complete causal explanation.

It may be said, of course, that our dissatisfaction with purposive explanation is like that of a philosopher who looks for a justification of induction; he has been told by Strawson[14] and others that inductive argument is simply one kind of argument and that it is wrong to try to justify it or judge it in terms of deductive argument, but he remains dissatisfied with it. Whether or not the comparison with induction is apt, however, it is certainly the case that purposive explanation of human action is the best that we can hope for; and if this conclusion seems unsatisfactory the alternatives provided by the determinist seem even more so, because they suggest that our ordinary assumptions about ourselves and our actions are radically misleading.

6. CONCLUSION

We have argued that to respect a person as an end is to take his conduct seriously and to assume that it is to be explained purposively, where that is regarded as equivalent to assuming that the person is morally responsible. The necessary connexions between being a person, being purposive and being morally responsible are shown in the facts that if we can establish that a specific individual is not in the full sense a person—that he is mentally deficient or the like—then we do not regard him as morally responsible; and if we can show that specific actions of persons in the full sense do not reflect the exercise of purposiveness—that they were done in ignorance, say, or as the result of constraint—then we do not regard their agent as being fully morally responsible for them. To argue in this way is to argue for the ultimacy of explanations of people's behaviour which make use of the concept of rational choice. So much seems to be a necessary feature of looking at action from the agent's standpoint.

There is also a spectator standpoint, however, from which we expect that all events, including human actions, will be open to causal explanations. There seems to be an incompatibility between the assumptions of the two standpoints, but some determinists have argued that it is only a *prima facie* incompatibility because desire can be given a causal analysis, and all purposive concepts can be analysed in terms of desire. We accepted the first premise, but rejected the second; decision or choice are concepts necessary to purposive explanation of human action, and such concepts cannot be analysed causally for epistemological reasons. Hence, this way out of the conflict of standpoints had to be rejected even before we

H

considered what must be the essential nature of choice if it is to be adequate for responsible action. The rejection of psychological determinism leaves the way open to physical determinism, which is at least free of logical difficulties. The physical determinist offers a causal explanation of the brain-states etc. which are alleged to be the physical determinants of the occurrence of choice. Some philosophers have argued that causal explanations of this nature are complementary to those in the purposive mode. But we have rejected this solution, and are forced to conclude that rational choice, and the concepts of action stemming from it, are not susceptible to complete causal explanation. In other words, if we accept the validity of the concept of rational will we must accept the possibility of undetermined choice, and with it an unavoidable incompleteness in our explanations of action. The only alternative is to accept a view which undermines the whole concept of responsible action.

CHAPTER V

RESPECT FOR PERSONS
AND META-ETHICS

1. THE LOGICAL STATUS OF 'RESPECT FOR PERSONS'

In Chapters I-III we argued that the attitude of *agape* or respect for persons is morally basic in that it gives rise to the supreme regulative principle of public and private morality. In this Chapter we shall attempt to discover the kind of meta-ethical* view which respect-for-persons morality permits or requires. As a preliminary we shall discuss the logical features which respect-for-persons morality possesses.

Throughout our argument we have regarded morality as concerned with an absolute or overriding claim—indeed, we have treated this as true by definition. Thus we hold that to say (truly or falsely) 'I morally ought to do A' is to say that such action is of paramount importance. The argument in Chapter III, Section 6, for example, explicitly depends on this conception of morality and in many other contexts we tacitly assume this view as a premise. It must be stressed that the overriding *claim* of what we morally ought to do is not the same as overriding *motivation* to do it. We shall refer to this important distinction later† but in the meantime simply note it and consider how far we can argue for the view that morality presents overriding claims. In the end, as we have said, we are making it a matter of definition that moral claims are overriding, but we can at least try to make the stipulation plausible. To do so it is necessary to argue for two propositions: that a moral claim always overrides an interest, and that a moral claim always overrides any other sort of claim, such as a legal duty.

* The meanings of the terms 'meta-ethics' and 'metaphysics of morality' to a great extent overlap. On the whole, 'meta-ethics' is used more where *logical* considerations are dominant, and 'metaphysics of morality' where wider metaphysical considerations are dominant. Thus, Chapter IV is more appropriately regarded as an exercise in the metaphysics of morality and Chapter V in meta-ethics. But the distinction is by no means clear in many cases, and we shall often use the terms interchangeably.

† See pp. 139-40.

To make it plausible that a moral claim always overrides an interest we must meet the following familiar sort of example. One person, X, promises to have lunch with another, Y, but subsequently receives an invitation from Z and learns that he will be offered a highly desirable post by him. We can stipulate that there will be no time to cancel the first lunch date. In this situation we might well hold that it would be *appropriate* for X to break his promise to Y, and so it may seem that a large interest can override a small moral claim.

But is this the only interpretation? If we suppose that X and Y are friends another explanation becomes possible. We can say that the relationship of friendship allows a certain moral give-and-take. If Y knew of the situation he would, if he were X's friend, waive the promise. Indeed, he might even feel offended if X did not presume on the friendship to break the promise in the circumstances. Hence, in this case, an interest would not override a moral claim, but rather a duty of friendship would override one of promise-keeping.

But this argument assumes that X and Y are friends. What if they are not? If the interest which X hopes to further is only a moderate one it is not clear that the moral claim *is* overridden; moral virtue is not to be had on the cheap. Suppose, however, that the interest is very large. If so, it may be that X's own interests are involved with those of others—his family, or the like—in which case he would have a duty to further their interests if he could. But let us stipulate (unplausibly) that even although X has expectations of large-scale advances in his interests these do not affect others at all. Do we now have a case of a large interest overriding a small duty? At this point it is tempting to say that if the interests are as important as all that they are not *simply* interests. If they take the form of a new and exciting job, or the like, they will *ipso facto* be the provision of opportunities for the self-development which we have argued is a claim of private morality. To make a dialectical move of this kind, of course, is merely to reassert in a disguised way that we are making it true by definition that a moral claim cannot be overridden by an interest; but it may also be to make the stipulation more plausible.

Let us now consider the second proposition—that a moral claim cannot be overridden by a legal or other claim. An argument for this proposition can be developed if we point out that to place moral claims on a par with other kinds is to make them simply one out of a large number of possible sets of claims competing for the attention of an agent. For example, it is not unknown for artists to speak of 'aesthetic conscience' and to regard this as something which may compete in its claims on the artist with those of moral conscience. Art may then be conceived as a form of activity which imposes claims on the artist by virtue of his participation in it. Again, there is something which is occasionally described as 'scientific integrity', and what seems to be meant by this expression is that the nature of scientific activity imposes on its participants claims which may on occasion compete with moral claims. Having once admitted the existence of autonomous aesthetic and scientific claims, however, we must admit claims imposed by any serious form of human activity, and the result is that morality will be confined to a narrow area of human experience—that concerned with such matters, say, as truth-telling and the regulation of sexual behaviour. It seems more plausible, however, to say that 'aesthetic conscience', 'scientific integrity' etc. refer simply to the *content* of what are for different people *prima facie* moral claims. We can then retain the concept of the overriding moral claim, while allowing that the content of the overriding claims may vary widely.[1]

The plausibility of the wide interpretation of 'moral' is best supported by considering the nature of the reasoning and deciding which takes place if we are faced with incompatible claims. Suppose that a person is faced with a conflict between the claims of his art and those of his family, or between those of the law of the land and his conscience. Here the situation arises for the artist because he asks himself what he ought above all to do. Similarly, the protester (if he is sincere) is concerned with whether his paramount duty lies in obeying the law of the land or in witnessing to his disapproval of it. In other words, in these situations the agent is searching to discover what has an overriding claim on him. We need a concept to cover this important and characteristic type of thinking, and so it is plausible to stipulate that the concept of 'morality' should be used for such thinking and deciding. In saying, therefore, that respect for persons is the basic *moral* principle of our society and that all other moral judgements can be derived from it, we are by definition speaking about claims regarded as overriding.

Having defended our stipulation that morality is overriding against two possible counter-attacks we shall now consider the second of the logical features which, we hold, characterizes a morality of respect for persons, and perhaps all morality: that of universalizability.

We first mentioned universalizability in Chapter II, in our discussion of utilitarianism. There we distinguished between the logical and the moral senses of the word 'universalizability', and said that logical universalizability was a feature of rules and reasons. We expressed the principle of logical universalizability as follows: where a rule or reason applies it must be followed on every occasion without discrimination unless some criterion of difference can be produced. Logical universalizability, then, as applied to rules and reasons, simply means 'general application', and the universalizability (in this sense) of rules and reasons follows logically from the fact that, whether wide or narrow in their scope, they are already in general terms.

We now wish to raise the question whether all particular moral judgements must be supported by rules or reasons. By a particular moral judgement we mean one which is couched entirely in particular terms, as for example, 'I ought to go and see Mrs Jones'. The question, then, is whether a person can intelligibly say just this, and be unable to 'back it up' by reference to a rule ('People ought to visit lonely old ladies') or a reason ('Because she is old and lonely'). We hold that this does not seem an intelligible possibility.[2] Of course, a moral agent may be unable to formulate his reasons immediately if the situation is complex, but he must have reasons which could in time be produced if what he says is to be comprehensible.

We can express this requirement—that all particular moral judgements should be related to a reason or rule—by distinguishing a third sense of 'universalizability' which applies only to particular judgements. This sense is logical rather than moral. It differs from the sense of 'logical universalizability' which applies to rules and reasons in that the latter means 'general application', whereas the sense which applies to particular moral judgements means 'capable of being *made* of general application'. Thus if we insist that a particular judgement like 'I ought to go and see Mrs Jones' is logically universalizable, we mean that there are features of the particular situation which support the moral judgement in this case and which would therefore give rise to similar judgements in other cases with the same features. Our view, then, is that all particular moral judgements must be universalizable in this third sense.

How can we defend the assertion of the universalizability (in the third sense) of particular moral judgements? We said rather vaguely above that a particular moral judgement which is not thus universalizable does not seem to make sense. But it is not an obvious consequence of the logical form of such judgements that they be universalizable, in the way that rules and reasons must be of general application in virtue of their form. Nor does the universalizability (in the third sense) of particular moral judgements follow from the mere definition of the word 'ought' as Peters suggests when he says: '. . . the notion of "ought" is more or less equivalent to the notion of there being reasons for something'.[3] For, if this were so, we could not use the same word 'ought' in a statement of an ultimate principle, where *ex hypothesi* there is nothing beyond it in terms of which reasons for the 'ought' might be given.

We can defend the thesis of the universalizability of particular judgements more satisfactorily if we say that we necessarily regard morality as possessing some kind of *coherence*. If we did not regard it in this light we would have to allow the possibility of infinite numbers of unconnected judgements which could be called 'moral', and this does not seem an intelligible notion. In other words, we cannot understand the idea of a moral judgement which cannot be linked with others and so (as it were) 'made sense of'. And if anyone says that *he* makes moral judgements of the form 'I ought to call on Mrs Jones', and sees no need to back them up with reasons or rules, our reply would be that he does not understand the kind of thing we have in mind when we speak of morality.

It will be seen that this insistence on the universalizability of particular moral judgements embodies a *preference* for coherence as against incoherence, the rational as against the irrational. Thus our account of the nature of morality is not value-neutral, but itself embodies valuations, at least when it is taken together with the stipulation that morality is overriding. This is in no way a defect. Any attempt to give an account of the nature of morality will embody some valuations—there is no such thing as *the* concept of morality awaiting detached examination from a neutral standpoint.[4]

The third logical feature of morality on which we wish to lay stress is that it is in some sense *practical*, or closely connected with action. The general notion of the practicality of morality does not need defence—it is obvious that the 'ordinary moral judgements' of Chapters I-III are to do with action in some way. Let us try to consider further in what way we regard morality as practical.

First of all it may be said that morality is practical in the obvious sense that its *subject-matter* is action—it is about what we ought to do. Secondly, it seems to be practical in a rather stronger sense— moral judgements seem in some way to *lead* to action. Thus there would be something odd and needing to be explained about a man who said 'We ought to be kind' or 'We ought to develop ourselves' and did nothing about it. This idea, that moral judgements lead to action in some sense, is not as such controversial although, as we shall see, there can be different interpretations of it. But thirdly —and this point seems to conflict with the second—it is a fact that sometimes a man may sincerely say that he ought to do some- thing, and yet not do it. There have been views in the history of philosophy which have stated or implied that if one really knows what one ought to do, if one knows the good, one will always do it. But these views seem at least to be incompatible with a familiar phenomenon of our everyday moral experience—the phenomenon we refer to as 'weakness of will'. Of course, it may be that the phenomenon of moral weakness is not what it seems to be. But it is at any rate clear that any account of the practicality of morality must accommodate it in some form or other. Hence, the third logical feature of morality which we wish to emphasise is practi- cality, but practicality so analysed as to make room for weakness.

The fourth feature of morality on which we shall lay stress is that of *objectivity*. By this we mean that moral judgements are correct or incorrect, true or false, and fall into the logical category of expressions of belief. This is the most controversial feature of our account of the nature of morality, and indeed some views of moral- ity do not make objectivity a logical feature of it at all. But we shall insist that objectivity is a feature at least of the morality character- ized in terms of respect for persons. For the time being we shall not argue for this thesis as such, but shall simply list some of the factors which might lead philosophers to insist that objectivity is a feature of morality. In subsequent sections we shall hope to show that, if we are to do justice to these factors in the form in which they are embodied in the respect for persons morality, we *must* regard morality as objective in the sense laid down above (which is what we shall mean by 'objectivity' from now on).

The first factor which leads philosophers to maintain that morality is objective is that morality seems to be a rational mode of activity rather than an arbitrary one. Moral agents are expected to support their judgements and conduct with reasons, to answer such questions as 'Why did you do that?' or 'Why did you speak in that tone of voice?' In other words, the defence 'I just happened to feel like it' is not considered a moral defence because it smacks of arbitrariness. A connected aspect of the rationality of morality is that we look for *consistency* in moral conduct. There are two relevant sorts of consistency in this context: between words and deeds, and between words and words or deeds and deeds over a period of time. We expect that what people say about morality should be reflected at least to some extent in their moral conduct, and we expect that what they say about morality or what they do should reflect stable policies rather than vary like the daily weather. People do, of course, change their minds on moral questions, but we do look for roughly continuous moral policies, and we look for them because we expect morality to be rational. (This demand for rationality in morality has already been mentioned in our discussion of universalizability.) Now some philosophers argue that we cannot make sense of the presupposition that morality is rational unless we ascribe objectivity to morality. As we shall see in the next section, those who think that objectivity is not required by rationality are interpreting rationality in too weak a fashion to meet the requirements of respect-for-persons morality.

The second (although related) factor which leads philosophers to ascribe objectivity to moral judgements is the existence of moral disagreement. Arguing on moral matters is a common activity, but it would not make sense to have a moral argument if there were no disagreement about which to argue, any more than one can have an argument between two men because one thinks that Edinburgh is the most beautiful city in Scotland and the other thinks that Oxford is the most beautiful city in England. People can and do talk at cross-purposes and *discover* that they do not in fact disagree, but this certainly is not the general situation in moral arguments. It may also be the case that some moral disagreements cannot be resolved, but, if this is the case, then disagreement certainly exists. But if disagreement exists, it is plausible to insist that there must be some objective fact which the disagreement is about. Again, of course, there is the possibility of differing accounts of the nature of moral disagreement—and this we shall discuss in the next section—but in the meantime we maintain only that the existence of moral disagreement may render plausible the introduction of the notion of the objectivity of morality.

The third factor which points to objectivity is what we may call moral seriousness. People do feel that the moral conduct of themselves and others matters—some would say matters supremely. It is easy to provide real life examples of moral seriousness, of people sacrificing their inclinations, major interests and even their lives for moral principles. Again, real life and literature abound with instances of the agonies men may go through in deciding what they morally ought to do, and, when they have decided, in doing it. Consider, for example, the literary and philosophical analyses which Existentialists provide of the concept of 'anguish'. Now it seems difficult to make sense of moral seriousness unless we presuppose that the agent thinks there is something objective which he is trying to identify in his moral judgement and embody in his conduct—though once again the plausibility of this assertion depends on what account we give of moral seriousness.

We have, then, three factors which may lead philosophers to ascribe objectivity to morality—its rationality, moral disagreement and moral seriousness. In the next section, in the course of our discussion of Hare, we shall show how these factors must be interpreted if they are to meet the requirements of respect-for-persons morality, and shall argue that if they are interpreted in this way morality must be regarded as objective.

Assuming, then, that we have identified the main logical features of the morality of respect for persons—that it is overriding, universalizable, practical and objective—we shall go on to decide what meta-ethical view respect for persons requires or permits.

2. THE COMMITMENT THEORY

One general type of theory stating a meta-ethics can be called the 'commitment theory'. This theory can be found in the writings of Existentialists, where it is often developed from the point of view of the phenomenology of complex moral situations. It is also to be found in the writings of Hare, where it is stated as a meta-ethical theory. In brief, the theory is to the effect that in the end the moral agent simply chooses his ultimate moral principles, and to choose one's moral principles is to commit oneself to the sort of conduct which the principles enjoin. If we regard this as a meta-ethics of the outlook we outlined in Chapters I-III it will mean that agents whose morality is that of respect for persons have simply chosen this as their ultimate moral principle and in so doing have committed themselves to conduct of the general kind we have outlined. On this meta-ethics an expression such as 'I ought to respect persons' will be seen as a command addressed to oneself or (since the split in personality suggested by self-command is a puzzling idea) as an expression of firm intention. Now if we construe a moral judgement on the lines of a statement of intention we shall have to hold that a man who says 'I ought to do such and such' and then does the opposite is either insincere or does not in fact have the moral view when it comes to act; and exponents of the commitment view have been happy with this consequence.

This view of morality has several advantages, some of which have been brought out by Hare, whose version of the commitment theory we shall discuss. In the first place—and this point is stressed by Hare—the theory enables us to do justice to the claim of practicality which we discussed earlier. Indeed, the theory seeks to establish that there is a *logical* connexion between judgement and action, a view commonly known as the thesis of prescriptivity.* In the second place, it appeals to the cynical, 'actions speak louder than words' streak in everyone. In view of these advantages (and there may be others) it is not surprising that the theory has been widely accepted. It has also been widely criticized, however, and we shall now consider some criticisms, and the extent to which they prevent the theory from providing an adequate meta-ethical account of the morality of respect for persons.

The commitment theory has no difficulty in coping with the first two logical features of the morality of respect for persons. Hare stresses that moral judgements are overriding, and that they are universalizable. His emphasis on universalizability is in fact one of the striking aspects of his theory, although we shall argue that he places too much weight on it and tries to make it serve also for what we regard as the separate feature of objectivity.

---

* It should be noted that the term 'prescriptivity' is sometimes used as a synonym for 'practicality'. This use of the term is misleading, however, for prescriptivity is only one out of several possible accounts of how morality is practical; the 'good reasons' theory and non-naturalism each have their own account to give of practicality.

It will be seen that the commitment theory—in all its versions—lacks *objectivity*. This does not, however, rule it out without further discussion as an account of the metaphysics of the respect-for-persons morality. For (as we said in the previous section) our reason for insisting that the respect-for-persons morality is objective is that we wish to accommodate three other features which are essential to that view of morality: the rationality (as opposed to arbitrariness) of morality, the existence of moral disagreement, and the seriousness with which morality is regarded. If then the commitment theory can accommodate these features in an adequate form without introducing objectivity, it is still a possible metaphysical account of respect-for-persons morality. We must now consider how far it can do this.

Hare holds that he does full justice to the *rationality* of morality by his stress on universalizability.[5] He maintains that reasons must be given for particular decisions, in terms of the factors on which the moral judgement is grounded, and that these reasons require the same moral judgement in all cases where they obtain. Thus, in his view, moral judgements are not arbitrary (in the sense that they follow no principles). Indeed, Hare might say that his view depicts morality as objective not in our 'strong' sense but in the only sense which really matters—the sense in which an examiner is said to be objective if his judgements from day to day are based on the same factors.

But this account of the rationality of moral judgements shows only how the particular judgement may be said to be rational. The choice of one general rule rather than another is still an arbitrary matter. Certainly, on this account, I must back up my judgement that I ought to put my debtor into prison with the general rule that all creditors ought to put their debtors into prison. And if I am prepared to do this I cannot, on Hare's terms, be accused of irrationality. But there is surely more to rational behaviour than consistency. Hare thinks that in practice people will not be prepared to prescribe rules that go against their interests, and dubs those who are prepared to do this 'fanatics'.[6] But he cannot consistently say that the fanatics are mistaken in their views; he can only provide methods whereby those who oppose them can seek to weaken their influence. This is done by robbing them of the support of the non-fanatical, who will be swayed by an argument from generalized self-interest.

Now whatever the merits and demerits of this method of dealing with an opponent, it is clear that the most it can do is to change the opponent's view by showing it to be inconsistent with other views he holds. It does not prove him wrong, and if he is a fanatic he is not even shown to be inconsistent. In other words, Hare's account of the rationality of morality is simply in terms of the coherence which arises from universalizability. But the demand that morality should not be *arbitrary* goes further than this. For if a man's moral views cannot be justified in the end except insofar as they form a coherent system among themselves, and cannot be criticized except on grounds of inconsistency, surely taken as a whole they must still be regarded as arbitrary.

Hare might reply to this charge by saying that arbitrariness of this kind cannot be seen as a defect peculiar to his view of morality; on the contrary, it is a necessary feature of morality whatever one's view of its nature. For on any view justification has to stop some-where. It does not make sense always to go on asking for justifica-tion, so if someone holds that a certain principle, such as respect for persons, is true and ultimate, he also must be committed to a judgement—an expression of belief in his case—which is arbitrary in the sense that it cannot be supported. What is so different, as far as arbitrariness goes, between a set of ultimate commitments and a set of ultimate beliefs, which, just because they are ultimate, cannot be backed up in any way?

Now there are really two points we must consider in answering this question. One is the thesis that a belief which is said to be ultimate cannot be justified, and the other is the suggestion that ultimate beliefs are as arbitrary as ultimate commitments. But neither of these points holds without qualification. It is perhaps true (to take the first point) that the ultimate principles of a system cannot be justified from within the system; but it would not follow that no external method of justification is possible. Even if external justification is not possible, however, it is clear (to move to the second point) that ultimate beliefs are not arbitrary in the same sense as ultimate commitments. For the important feature of belief is that it is true or false in virtue of facts which hold inde-pendently of us, whereas to say that something is arbitrary suggests rather that it is settled by our *fiat*. It is therefore possible to agree that 'justification has to stop somewhere' while at the same time stressing the difference between a belief, which is arbitrary only in the sense that it cannot be further justified, and a decision, which is arbitrary in the proper sense of being dependent entirely on our will. The aspect of rationality, then, to which Hare's theory cannot do justice is the notion of morality as something which we cannot please ourselves about and which is independent of our choices; and non-arbitrariness in this sense does not merely require objectivity—it is *identical* with it.

The question which arises now is whether the respect-for-persons morality requires the strong sense of non-arbitrariness, the notion that morality is discovered rather than chosen. It seems clear that it does. For if we hold respect for persons as our ultimate moral principle we feel we must adhere to this; we do not feel, as we would on Hare's theory, that we would have been able to choose another principle instead. The case is rather that the principle presents itself to us as the right one, without our having any say in the matter. We are responding to something outside ourselves, as it were, and this is the situation of belief, which is the reflection of something seen as independent of the believer. We cannot but see things as we see them, morally or otherwise. This does not mean that we cannot change our minds, but only that we cannot choose to do so. Our moral judgements are properly to be described as beliefs and not as choices, and they are not arbitrary in the sense that *we* could have made them otherwise.

Now this account of the phenomenology of moral judgement would be rejected by many, as embodying some kind of self-deception—in fact it might well be looked on as the essence of *mauvaise foi*. The Existentialists' concept of *mauvaise foi* may be defined as the pretence that one is determined when in fact one has to choose, and they apply this necessity of choice not only to action but also to moral judgement. Thus Sartre speaks of a young man *making* the law for himself in a moral dilemma,[7] where it seems more appropriate to say that he thought on reflection that the right decision would be such-and-such, that it was borne in on him, appeared to him, etc. We would however grant that there are situations where a man may remain utterly baffled, but 'plump' quite arbitrarily for one alternative or the other because he has to make a decision. But this kind of case should not be used to depict our normal state of mind when making a moral judgement. For when a man has to make such an arbitrary choice, we would say that this is to be *contrasted* with ordinary moral judgement, rather

than equated with it. Thus although in this case we may say of him
'He decided to do such-and-such', we would not say 'He decided
that he ought to do such-and-such'. Moreover, it should be stressed
that this kind of activity is not even what we normally mean by
'choice'. It is more a case of 'picking' than of 'choosing', for choice
normally presupposes some judgement that what is chosen is
better than the alternatives.

We conclude, then, that respect-for-persons morality must be
seen as non-arbitrary in the strong sense which is identical with
objectivity, and so cannot be accommodated by the commitment
theory.

The second factor which seemed to us relevant to the claim that
the morality of respect for persons is objective was that people
disagree over moral questions and discuss the issues involved. Can
the commitment theorist give an account of moral discussion which
is non-objective but nevertheless adequate to respect-for-persons
morality?

Consider first what 'moral discussion' implies. Peters assumes,
in effect, that its existence implies that morality is objective; for
he maintains that to give reasons 'is to assume that truth and error
are possible about the matter under discussion. For how could
discussion have any point without such an assumption?'[8] But this
is not true without qualification. If, for instance, the participants
(or some of them) already hold a certain position on the matter at
issue, a discussion might have the status of a *debate*, a process of
which the object is to win others over to one's point of view rather
than necessarily to arrive at the truth of the matter. The motive
for securing this agreement might be that it was essential for the
implementation of a policy. Or again, a wish that others should
think likewise might be embodied in the attitude or stance adopted.
But if participants in a discussion do not have firm views, but are
trying to decide what to think, it seems very difficult to account for
the seriousness with which this is done without seeing it as a *joint
investigation*, a procedure which aims at finding out the truth of
some matter. As in the case of the individual moral agent's discussion with himself, participants in such a discussion are not content
merely to end uncertainty by arriving somehow at a conclusion—by
tossing a coin, for example. Nor are they content simply to tease
out the consequences of other views they may hold, and say 'If
we hang on to that, we must say such-and-such about this'. Charac-

teristically, a serious discussion will question such assumptions in their turn; and while it is true that such questioning brings us to a point where discussion has to stop, it does not bring us to a point where people are willing to conclude: 'Here it doesn't matter what we say'.

Our conclusion about moral discussion, then, is that it may be of two kinds—joint investigation and debate. On the commitment theory it must be construed as a debate, since joint investigation assumes (what the commitment theory excludes) that there is truth and falsity in the matter under moral discussion. But debate is incompatible with seriousness in discussion, and seriousness in discussion is surely required by respect-for-persons morality (or perhaps any morality). It follows that the commitment theory cannot give an account of moral discussion adequate to respect-for-persons morality.

The third factor which led us to ascribe objectivity to the morality of respect for persons was that of moral seriousness. Can the commitment theorist give an account of moral seriousness of a kind appropriate to the moral outlook we are considering?

This question is in fact partly answered already, since we have just asserted that the commitment theorist cannot do justice to the seriousness required in moral discussion. But the commitment theorist might reply that moral seriousness on his view is expressed in the agent's emotional reaction to the responsibility of choosing his own morality. For example, the Existentialists lay stress on the anguish of a moral agent in trying to decide what to do. Now this is a plausible account of the difficulties an agent may have in complex situations, but it is not clear that a commitment theorist can account for it in terms of his theory. For anguish seems to presuppose that there is a *right* choice to be made (if we but knew what it was). There is no particular difficulty about making a choice; if there is nothing to go by and no question of the right or wrong choice, the agent can spin a coin. But trying to make the right choice presupposes the notion of belief—if not the belief that the choice one makes is the right choice, at least the belief that there is such a thing as the right choice, which is fixed as such independently of my choosing it. And this is the essence of objectivity. Moreover, the belief that there is a right choice and a wrong one seems necessary to explain, not only Existentialist anguish, but the general notion of moral seriousness. For how can it be said to *matter* what one decides, unless it is possible that one might make the wrong decision? But the commitment theorist cannot speak of right and wrong decision. As we have seen, he holds that in the end we just make a decision—we plump. It seems that for him there is nothing to be serious about. He cannot therefore account for the third factor which is required by the morality of respect for persons, and which argues for objectivity.

Our discussion of the commitment theory has so far confirmed that objectivity in the strong sense is required by respect-for-persons morality. Moral judgements are to be construed as the expressions of belief—as discoveries rather than as choices—because only by so depicting them can we do justice to the connected points that morality so understood is a rational activity in which we try through serious discussion with ourselves or others to reach the correct judgement about what we ought to do. A commitment theory is inadequate to morality so described because it holds that in the end morality is a matter of arbitrary decision.

Now we have in fact said enough to rule out the possibility that an adequate meta-ethical view of respect for persons can be provided by the commitment theory. But we wish to discuss the account which the commitment theory provides of practicality, because such a view is of considerable interest for its own sake and also lays the foundation for an account of practicality appropriate to respect-for-persons morality.

The nature of practicality is discussed by commitment theorists in terms of the thesis of prescriptivity—that there is a logical connexion between moral judgement and action—and the thesis is often introduced by posing the question of the criteria of assent to a moral rule. Now while we too shall adopt this approach to the thesis of prescriptivity we must point out that it carries with it certain possibilities of confusion. One of these is that the question is posed in terms of assent to a *rule*, whereas the real rub concerning the practicality of moral judgements seems to arise in the particular situation, as we shall shortly demonstrate. The second possibility of confusion seems to arise over the word 'assent', which carries with it suggestions of obedience. For if the notion of obedience is built into the very posing of the question of what it is to hold a moral belief then the commitment theorist is on the way to begging the question. We must therefore make clear from the outset that in speaking of criteria of assent we shall mean no more than in speak-

I

ing of criteria of belief—namely, the criteria for saying truly of someone that he thinks he ought to do so-and-so. Thirdly, there remains the possibility of confusion over the sense of the word 'criteria'. It can be given a logical meaning or an empirical meaning; thus in speaking of the criteria for holding a moral belief, we may be expounding either what it *means* to say someone holds a moral belief or what *happens when* someone holds a moral belief which can serve as an index of his holding it. This distinction is not one which is made sharply in ordinary talk, so in our general survey of the relationship between moral belief and action we shall not press it. But philosophers who attempt to write conativeness into the analysis of moral judgements naturally think of criteria in logical terms, as will be apparent.

We shall begin with a modification of the theory which cannot legitimately be construed as a criticism. Sometimes moral rules clash, and the fact that a person is acting in terms of one moral rule can hardly be used as evidence that he does not genuinely assent to another, if he believes that the first is more appropriate in his situation. For instance, a person may be in a situation in which the rule about promise-keeping and the rule about truth-telling both apply, but it is not possible to act in terms of both. To act in terms of one rather than of the other is not here to offer evidence that the other is not also held as a moral rule.

The most common criticism of the theory is based on what is often said to be one of its main merits—the fact that it is able to establish a logical connexion between judgement and action. The criticism is that the commitment theory makes the connexion between moral belief and action so close that no room can be found for weakness of will, and weakness of will, as we stressed in Section 1, is a phenomenon of the moral life which any theory must take into account. We described weakness of will in general terms as knowing what we ought to do yet failing to do it. Under this general description, however, are sometimes included phenomena which are not cases of *weakness* in the strict sense. Consider first what may be called *ignorance in the particular situation*.

Ignorance in the particular situation may be said to occur when a person, if explicitly asked whether or not he accepts a particular moral rule, replies in the affirmative, but yet seems unaware that the rule applies to a given situation in which he finds himself. Now there may be several kinds of ignorance about the particular case, and the first can be called lack of perceptiveness. A man may hold some general principle, but fail to see its application in a particular case because he lacks an 'eye' for the complexities of morality. For example, he may hold that one should not hurt people's feelings, but fail to see that some clumsy piece of humiliating charity will have just that effect. Failure of this kind to put one's moral principles into practice cannot be construed as moral weakness at all (Aristotle would have called it a lapse of practical wisdom). It may, of course, be culpable; we certainly feel remorseful sometimes because we did not at the time see an action of our own in the appropriate light. Again, we feel that it is a moral agent's business to cultivate the 'eye' which is required. But, although it may be culpable as a case of ignorance in the particular situation, it does not seem to be genuinely a case of *moral weakness*, and hence it does not create a difficulty for the commitment theory about the relation between judgement and action.

A second case of ignorance in the particular situation may be said to occur when a person is in the grip of a morally blinding emotion. Aristotle compares this kind of ignorance with drunkenness, when a man can say things without knowing what they mean—presumably he wishes to allow for the fact that a man can say 'I know I oughtn't to do this' while actually doing it.[9] Now it is certainly the case that a man can get into a state of this kind in which his words are not to be taken seriously, and no doubt he is culpable for allowing himself to get into this state, but it does not seem plausible to regard this as a case of moral weakness in the strict sense. Hence, once again, it does not constitute a difficulty for the commitment theory.

There is, however, a third case of ignorance in the particular situation which is more troublesome for the commitment theory—the case of self-deception. Sometimes, when a person claims to subscribe to a rule, but fails to see that it applies in the particular situation in which he finds himself, we may question his sincerity with us or himself. It is all too easy to *refuse* to realize that a rule applies in a particular situation—not to allow oneself to see that one is committed. In such cases the agent may describe himself afterwards as 'really having known all along'. And it seems arguable that it is only when an agent can describe himself as having known all along that we have a genuine instance of weakness of will. It is therefore important in considering cases of particular ignorance to distinguish self-deception from Aristotle's morally blinding emotion. How far can the commitment theorist explain the phenomenon of self-deception in terms of his theory?

He could contest the claim that in self-deception it is possible for the agent to say 'I knew all along'. Self-deception (the commitment theorist might argue) arises because the agent lacks a certain sort of moral clear-sightedness, but clear-sightedness of this sort depends on the presence of virtues which require slow cultivation; and if the agent lacks these it is not correct to say that he 'knew all along'. His self-deception is really either a case of lack of perceptiveness or one of emotional dazzlement. If this reply were accepted, self-deception could not be regarded as a case of weakness in any sense which would raise impossible difficulties for the commitment theory.

We have then three types of ignorance about the moral nature of a particular situation: ignorance caused by lack of perceptiveness, the dazzlement caused by emotion, and self-deception. All these may be culpable ignorances which do not excuse the action, but only the last presents even a *prima facie* difficulty concerning the relation between moral judgement and action, as it is only in this case that it is even plausible to say that the agent knew at the time what he ought to do but did something else. Yet the sense in which a self-deceiver can be said to 'know at the time' is problematic and cannot constitute a crucial objection to the commitment theory. We may say, then, that while ignorance in the particular situation is often loosely called 'weakness of will', it does not seem to be properly a form of it. Hence Aristotle, who discusses ignorance in the particular situation, does not seem to have any conception of weakness at all in the strict sense; he simply refines and amplifies the Socratic paradox that virtue is knowledge. His views are therefore acceptable to commitment theorists. But, unlike Aristotle, we assume that there are cases of weakness where ignorance is not in question and we shall now consider how far the commitment theorist can explain them. Relevant in this context is the concept of trying.

The concept of trying has several uses but common to them all is the idea of more or less obstructed doing. For example, if we see a person behaving in a manner the significance of which is not clear to us we may ask simply, 'What are you doing?' If, however, we ask 'What are you *trying* to do?' we convey not only our puzzlement about what he is doing but also our suspicion that he may be having difficulty in doing it. Again, if an agent has failed in what he was doing he may say, 'Well, that was what I was *trying* to do anyway', at once identifying the action and admitting that it has been in some way obstructed. Indeed, the concept of trying is so closely tied to suggestions of obstruction or difficulty that we allow that a person may be said to try things which he believes to be causally impossible. Now it is the fact that trying is necessarily a more or less obstructed doing that makes it a suitable concept to serve as a bridge between acceptance of a moral rule and action. If a person can be said to hold a rule as a moral rule it must be true of him that he at least tried to keep to it in situations of difficulty or temptation. One cannot always succeed, but one can always try.

Where the notion of 'trying', interpreted as a more or less obstructed doing, is applied to moral action it is obviously connected with the notion of making an effort of will. It is presupposed that at times one's adherence to a moral rule is upset. Now in the end the rule may be disregarded but, on the commitment theory, we can say of a person that he accepts the rule provided that some sort of effort of will was made towards resisting the temptation, and guilt was experienced if the effort of will was not in the end sufficient. This seems to be the central case of moral weakness, and it is arguable that the commitment theory can accommodate it.

But if the commitment theorist is to employ this analysis of moral weakness, he must meet an obvious objection to it. His argument requires the premise that one cannot always succeed but one can always try. This suggests that we are not to blame for what we do as a result of moral weakness, on the ground that no one can be blamed for failure to do what he cannot do. But we do blame people for moral weakness—we blame them not only for not trying, but also for trying and not succeeding. To answer this we may consider the role of the virtues. In discussing the virtues in Chapter III we argued that many virtues have the function of enabling a person to withstand a special temptation. We can now suggest that it is lack of some virtue which makes a man's efforts of will unsuccessful. He can be blamed for his failure, not because he could on this occasion have succeeded, but because his failure is thought to be due to the lack of a quality which it has been possible for him to acquire. Moreover, we think a virtue can be acquired by trying as well as by succeeding—'the more you try the easier it gets' is the kind of thing said to children.

But this account of moral weakness still does not do justice to some of the situations in which a man knows what he ought to do but does not do it—situations which are again often loosely called situations of moral weakness, but are more accurately to be described as cases of *perversity*. Consider that it does seem to be the case that we often feel we could have resisted the temptation on that particular occasion if we had tried a little harder. Certainly, there is no way of telling when this is true, but it is surely unplausible to hold that it is never true. Now if it is sometimes true, it seems reasonable to describe these occasions of weakness as occasions when the agent is consenting to do what he thinks he ought not to do—albeit after a struggle. And if it is admitted that a man may thus consent, why should it be denied that he may perversely decide to do what he thinks he ought not to do—as certainly seems to happen? We might in fact arrange the cases in which it can be said that a man knew what he ought to do but did not do it in a kind of order of effort. At one end of the scale are cases where the agent tried as hard as he could but still failed. At the other end are the cases where no effort at all is made. In between are the cases where some effort is made but where we feel inclined to say that the man could have succeeded if he had 'really tried'. Now nomenclature for this scale, as we have indicated, is not always standard: some would call the whole range 'weakness'. But even if one prefers to distinguish between weakness and perversity there seems to be no sharp dividing line between them. What is more important than the terminology, however, is the difficulty which the perversity end of the scale creates for the commitment theory. For if it does make sense to suppose, not only that a man may try and fail to live up to his moral beliefs, but also that he may deliberately flout them, then we have a serious objection to the commitment theory; doubt is cast on the nature of the logical connexion it seeks to establish between moral belief and action.

The conclusion of this discussion of weakness of will, then, is that three separate, although overlapping, phenomena are often loosely referred to as 'moral weakness'. Of these, ignorance in the particular situation is not strictly a case of weakness (unless *perhaps* in the form of self-deception), and hence does not constitute an objection to the commitment theory; moral weakness proper can be accommodated in the commitment theory by means of the concept of trying; but the existence of perversity is a crucial objection to the commitment theory.

We have been considering how far the commitment theory can provide an adequate meta-ethical or metaphysical account of morality as described in our first three chapters. The upshot is that it cannot do so at all. It is unable to do justice to objectivity in the strong sense required by a morality of respect for persons since it is incompatible with the notion that a moral judgement expresses a *belief* about the correct decision to make. And its failure to accommodate the phenomenon of perversity may make it inadequate as an account of any morality whatsoever.

3. NATURALISM

In our discussion of the commitment theory it emerged that the morality of respect for persons requires objectivity; moral judgements had to be construed as the expressions of belief that certain actions are right or wrong. Now if we adopt the metaphysics of naturalism we can do justice to objectivity so understood. For a metaphysics of morals is naturalistic if it reduces moral judgements to some other kind of judgement. For example, we might, by definition, reduce the question of what I ought to do to the question of what is pleasurable for me—basically a psychological question, but one also involving other kinds of empirical knowledge about the likely results of various policies. On the naturalistic view, therefore, moral knowledge is not *sui generis* but is a branch of some other kind of knowledge; and in this sense naturalistic theories deny the independence of morality. If then we can provide a naturalistic meta-ethics for 'One ought to respect persons' we shall be arguing that the 'ought' in the principle is to be analysed in some 'external' way—in terms, say, of what may produce pleasure or profit or be in accordance with God's will. In other words, a naturalistic account of objectivity allows us to say (as we require for our purposes) that a moral judgement expresses a belief which is true or false in virtue of some fact, but it commits us to saying that the fact is a non-moral one.

The meta-ethics of naturalism has been criticized in many respects. Consider first the most famous of all attacks on naturalism—that made by G. E. Moore in *Principia Ethica*.[10] In this book,

Moore describes what he calls the naturalistic fallacy, and although his account of it is very obscure, the fallacy seems to consist in the attempt to define the indefinable. He thinks that the word 'good' stands for a property which cannot be described in any other terms. Now it is not clear that the attempt to do this is a fallacy in the strict logical sense of the word. Moore talks as though naturalists attempt to equate things which are different, and quotes Butler's dictum 'everything is what it is and not another thing'—but this is to beg the question against the naturalist, who supposes (rightly or wrongly) that the definition does present us with 'what goodness is' and not 'another thing'. But whether or not Moore is correct in speaking of a fallacy rather than an error, his thesis has the effect of denying the possibility of a naturalistic meta-ethics in that it insulates morality from other forms of discourse and realms of knowledge.

The arguments which Moore brings to support his anti-naturalism (and hence his assertion of the autonomy of morality) are not very powerful. They amount to a request to consider the concepts in terms of which some philosopher seeks to define goodness, and see whether we have not got, in every case, an 'idea before the mind' which is distinct from that of goodness. This same idea is put more precisely in his notorious 'open question' test.[11] If we suppose 'good' to be defined in terms of pleasure, then 'Pleasure is good' becomes a tautology. But 'Pleasure is good' is not a tautology; it is an open question whether pleasure is good. And the same will hold for any other *definiens*.

The limitation of this argument is that Moore does not show why there can never be a tautology of the form 'X is good'. All he does is to suggest that certain *prima facie* plausible candidates for the *definiens* do not produce such tautologies. He has not ruled out the *possibility* of definition. To do this one would have to show that there is something about the word 'good' which precludes the possibility of defining it; and this is what Hare tries to do in the second argument against naturalism we shall consider.

Hare thinks that although Moore's argument was badly formulated his position as anti-naturalist was securely founded. He therefore attempts to restate Moore's argument in order to show why naturalism is untenable. For Hare, the error in naturalism is that of confusing the meaning of a value-word with the criteria for using it. Hare explains the meaning of the word 'good' in terms of its commendatory force. Thus when we say 'X is good', we mean, according to Hare, that X is to be commended for reasons Y and Z. For example, when we say that we had a good holiday we mean that the holiday is to be commended because the weather was warm, the hotel was comfortable, the company was diverting and so on. But if 'good' is *defined* as Y, Z, then 'good' means 'Y, Z,' and it becomes impossible to commend X for being Y and Z. Thus, if a 'good' holiday is defined as being one where the weather is warm, the hotel comfortable and so on, it adds nothing to say that a holiday with these characteristics is a good holiday. And in general, any definition of 'good' would prevent us from saying something that we do succeed in saying meaningfully in ordinary talk. This, then, is what Hare means by the naturalistic fallacy.[12]

The first thing that strikes one when considering this version of the naturalistic fallacy is that Hare is attacking a man of straw. Nobody would attempt to define a general word like 'good' in such specific terms as Hare suggests. But some very general definition— for example, one in terms of what we have reason to want—is a much more plausible candidate. Such a definition would not replace the specific criteria, but rather provide some ground for them. And Hare's talk of commending does not show why this type of general definition would be inadequate. For it is not at all obvious that, if we define 'good' as 'what we have reason to want', we shall feel deprived because we can no longer commend what we have reason to want by calling it good. On the contrary, we would normally be commending something *in saying* (whether truly or falsely) that people have reason to want it. Since commending can be carried out in making statements, the fact that the word 'good' is often and characteristically used to commend does not show that it cannot be used to make a statement. We think, then, that the attempt to refute naturalism by appeal to the commending function of evaluative language is unsuccessful.

A third type of argument against a naturalistic meta-ethics is often based on the practicality of moral judgements. It seems clear that, however it is to be analysed, there logically must be a practical dimension of moral judgements. Certainly, in our discussion of the commitment theory, we have already rejected the prescriptivist account of practicality on the grounds that the logical connexion it seeks to establish between moral judgement and action seems to rule out the possibility of perversity. But it is open to us to espouse a less extreme thesis of practicality and to maintain that the holding of a moral belief logically commits a moral agent, not necessarily to action itself, but to some measure of motivation or to a certain degree of inclination towards the appropriate action. Now it is not at first obvious that there is any property which necessarily carries a 'conative dimension' with it when attributed to some action or type of action. It always seems to make sense to say 'Why *do* anything?' or even 'Why care?' if an action is described in any terms other than those of the moral 'ought' itself, even if such questions might be eccentric in some cases.

What this amounts to can be seen by considering as an example a possible definition of the moral 'ought'. Some philosophers might say that the moral 'ought' is to be defined in terms of God's will. Thus, 'Persons ought to be respected' would mean 'It is God's will that persons be respected'. But then this does not seem to carry with it any implication that anyone must *do* anything. There seems no reason why someone who thinks something to be God's will logically must be motivated towards it, as is required by the nature of the moral 'ought'.

The difficulty with this argument, however, is that its scope is limited in a manner similar to that of the second anti-naturalist argument. In the discussion of the second argument we pointed out that if 'good' is defined in terms of what people have reason to want we do not obviously lose the commendatory force of value language, for to say of something that people have reason to want it would be to commend it. Thus the argument from the commendatory force of value language is plausible only against very specific and narrow definitions, such as those in terms of pleasure or God's will. In a similar way the argument from practicality is effective only against narrow definitions of 'ought' or 'good'. But if, once again, we define 'good' in terms of 'what people have reason to want' we do seem to have catered for the practical dimension of moral judgement. Let us therefore investigate this version of naturalism—which we shall call the 'good reasons' theory—in more detail, since it seems immune to the anti-naturalist arguments we have so far considered and can also offer us both objectivity in the strong sense and practicality.

According to this type of view if a thing is good a man has reason to pursue it, and thus to think that a thing is good is to think that one has reason to pursue it.[13] The analysis can be applied to moral goodness as well as to other kinds. Thus, if a person really thinks that a certain way of behaving is a good way, although he will not necessarily always act in this way, he will always acknowledge that he has good reason to act in this way. Insofar as a person really believes, say, that courage is a virtue, he must acknowledge that he has good reason for being courageous. This view leaves room for weakness of will, because the fact that one has a reason, even a very good reason, for being courageous, does not mean that one will always be courageous: one may also have a reason for being cowardly, namely, that one has a strong desire to run away from danger.

It may be objected that we have substituted 'being good' for 'doing as one ought', which has been our main topic. But the argument can be conducted equally well in terms either of a rule of behaviour or of a virtue. If we have chosen to conduct this discussion in terms of virtues it is because traditionally the view has been so discussed. Moreover, by discussing the virtues we hope to bring to light certain confusions which may have misled expounders of the 'good reasons' view.

The most important of these confusions arises out of the double ambiguity in the expression 'have a reason'. One ambiguity is that the phrase may imply that the man *knows* he has a reason, or it may not imply this. We shall try to use it always in the second of these senses, so that we can have a correspondence between a thing's being good without a man's knowing it and a man's having a reason to pursue the thing without knowing it. The other, and more important, ambiguity is that to have a reason can either mean to have a motive or to have a justification. To have a motive is to have some desire the fulfilment of which the action would promote, as when one speaks in a detective story of various people all having a motive for some crime. Thus the possession of a motive is a non-evaluative fact about the agent and the action. Justification, on the other hand, is an evaluative notion; if we say that a man is justified in doing something, we mean that some fact about his action made it (for example) an appropriate, sensible, praiseworthy, noble, thing to do. Thus the expression 'good reason' can be misleading; it may mean either 'strong motive' or 'abundant justification'. If the 'good reasons' account of the relation between judgement and action is to carry conviction it must be able to relate (as distinct from simply confusing) the two notions of 'strong motive' and 'abundant justification'.

Now it may be objected that these two notions are not as sharply distinguished as we have made them appear, on the grounds that a man must somehow have a motive to do what is appropriate, sensible, etc. But consider what is covered by this 'et cetera'. We included in the list of justifying qualities *moral* evaluations also, such as 'noble'. But whereas it may be reasonable to assume that a man must have a motive to do what is sensible, we cannot assume that he has a motive to do what is morally good without begging the whole question at issue, of the connexion between action and judgement of the good. We do not succeed in explaining this connexion by assuming that a man must have a motive to do what is good. But perhaps goodness may be *analysed in terms of* what a man has reason (in the sense of motive) to do. Now for our purposes an important advantage of such an analysis is that it enables us to ascribe objectivity to moral judgements. For objectivity implies the possibility of error and on this theory such a possibility can be accommodated, because a man does not always know what he has reason to do—and may indeed be mistaken about it—in that he does not always know what will bring him what he wants, or even what his wants are. It seems, then, as if the 'good reasons' theory can provide the objectivity which is required by a meta-ethical view adequate to respect for persons.

Moreover, as we noted earlier, the 'good reasons' theory can also provide us with practicality in the relevant sense. For if a man believes something to be good, he *ipso facto* thinks he has a motive-reason for doing it. The prescriptive type of view (exemplified by the commitment theory) tied the moral judgement logically to action, whereas the 'good reasons' view merely ties judgement to *reasons for* action. Thus the connexion between judgement and action is less tight on this view, and room is left for weakness of will. On the other hand, the 'good reasons' view does provide a logical and not merely contingent link between goodness and *wants*. It is not on this view just a fortunate fact about the world that people want what they think to be good—an empirical generalization to which we might find exceptions. The wish to avoid this merely contingent connexion between goodness and motivation is one reason why some philosophers opt for a full-blown prescriptive theory. But the 'good reasons' theory of practicality can avoid the difficulties both of a merely contingent connexion between goodness and motivation and of too tight a logical connexion between moral judgement and action. The main task, then, of someone who holds this view of moral judgement is not so much to explain the relationship of judgement to action—on his view this presents no problem—as to show that his account of the nature of goodness can reasonably be applied to those things which are actually thought to be morally good, in other words to show that morally good actions are such that men have motives for doing them.

Now if we hold that morally good actions are connected with respect for persons, on the lines sketched in our earlier chapters, it is not in fact particularly difficult to show that men have motives to be morally good—and the motives need not be simply what would normally be considered egoistic ones. For example, the motive of sympathy and the desire to be reasonable lead a man to respect others, while the desire for self-realization leads him to respect himself. But the trouble with this kind of account of morality seems to be that it leaves moral goodness too much on a par with other kinds. To see this, consider weakness of will again.

On the view of moral judgement suggested above, the man who believes one thing to be morally right but who nevertheless does something else is described as having good reasons both to be virtuous and to be non-virtuous. (For 'good reason' must mean simply 'strong motivation' if we are not to beg the question.) Thus, the close connexion with action which moral judgements possess may remain even when a man comes to act non-virtuously. But what is harder to explain on the 'good reasons' view is why a moral judgement should make a stronger claim to be acted upon than other value-judgements. In other words, it is difficult on this view to accommodate the overridingness which we argued to be a distinguishing feature of morality. For we should ordinarily say that there is something amiss when a man thinks that he morally ought to do something and yet does not do it, but on the 'good reasons' view there does not at first seem to be anything amiss. If the agent has strong motivation on either side, what account can be given of the special claim of moral goodness? Indeed, can moral goodness be distinguished from other kinds of goodness on the 'good reasons' theory?

The only answer to this problem, within the bounds of the 'good reasons' theory, would seem to be that to see something as morally good is to see it as affording not merely strong motivation but the *strongest* motivation—fulfilling more of one's wants or more intense wants than any alternative. On this view, the fault of the man who thinks he ought to do one thing but does another is that he is *irrational*, in that he does not look after his own best interests. The trouble with this solution, however, is that people who think they ought to do something often see it as against their best interests, and so, even if they are in fact mistaken about their best interests, they are not being irrational if they do what they believe they ought not to do. In any case it seems clear that they are often *not* mistaken, even allowing for the presence and strength of our 'other-regarding' motives. How far what is in a man's interests coincides with what is normally thought to be right depends very often on how prosperous the agent is.

Philosophers who go against the commonsense view and maintain that it is always in a man's interest to do what is right may be relying, as Butler does, on a *deus ex machina* who will right the balance in the end.[14] Or they may be confusing 'not always doing what is right' with 'always doing what is not right'. Thus Socrates in the *Republic*, perhaps disingenuously, presents the unjust man as one who always does what is not right.[15] It is clear that *this* policy, if it deserves the name, is not in a man's interests compared with justice; but it does not follow from this that the unjust man in the ordinary sense of the word—he who does not always do what is right—may not be better off than the just man.

Mrs P. Foot seems to make a similar mistake. Thus she says: 'The reason why it seems to some people so impossibly difficult to show that justice is more profitable than injustice is that they consider in isolation particular just acts.'[16] She presents the choice as one between uncompromising justice and an injustice seen in Platonic terms as involving cheating whenever it would profit one to do so. But the choice which presents itself in real life is between uncompromising justice and a policy of occasional injustice when great advantage accrues. A man who adopts the second policy is of course not a just man. But there is nothing irrational in his policy unless we suppose that by occasional unjust actions a man gets a bad reputation or makes it impossible for himself to be just on other occasions—gets out of training, as it were. But this view of the nature of a virtue, though it might be plausible as regards courage and temperance, seems most unplausible as applied to justice, which cannot be construed as any kind of skill.

It may be objected here, of course, that we have misunderstood the meaning of 'interest'. What is in a man's interest, it may be argued, is not simply what he wants, but rather what is good for him in the sense of 'good for his personal development' or something of that kind. And if 'interest' is understood in this way it is perfectly plausible to hold that in thinking an action is right a man thinks it is in his interest. But although interest can be construed in this way, we cannot both do this and use the notion of interest to explain the connexion between moral judgement and action. For the connexion between thinking something good for one in the above sense and doing it, like the connexion between thinking something justified and doing it, is as obscure as the connexion between thinking something right and doing it.

Or it might be maintained (now using 'interest' in what we may call its neutral sense) that a properly adjusted man, one in whom those motives which lead to good behaviour are very strong, would always find that duty and interest coincided. This may well be so, but it will not help with the present problem. For one thing, the man who is not properly adjusted will have no motive to behave in a way similar to that in which the properly adjusted man would behave; so to construe moral goodness in terms of what will appeal to the properly adjusted will not deal with the question of motivation. But more fundamentally, we cannot define moral goodness in terms of the interests of the properly adjusted, because in order to pick out the properly adjusted we must make use of a prior notion of moral goodness. That is to say, we regard the man in whom other-regarding motives are strong as properly adjusted only if we already approve of behaviour which is other-regarding. If we did not, we might think that the man who seemed to have no regard for others was properly adjusted—even if he were a very rare specimen.

We conclude, then, that while it may be possible to give a meta-ethical account of respect-for-persons morality in terms of the 'good reasons' theory the view is not without its difficulties. For the appropriate sense of 'good reason', as we have seen, is 'strong motivation', but on such an interpretation it seems difficult to accommodate the overriding nature of moral judgement.

4. NON-NATURALISM

We have rejected the commitment theory as a possible meta-ethics for respect-for-persons morality—it failed to do justice to the objectivity which is a feature of such a moral outlook. Naturalism, at least in the version which analyses morality in terms of what we have most reason to want, seemed more plausible as a meta-ethics, but it was not obviously compatible with the over-riding nature of moral claims as required by respect-for-persons morality. Let us therefore turn to a type of metaphysical view which goes almost by default in philosophical circles at the moment—the meta-ethics or metaphysics of non-naturalism.

According to this theory the principle of respect for persons will be true in virtue of a fact, but it will not be a fact of the natural world. Ways of describing this presupposed objective correlate of a moral judgement vary: some philosophers have spoken of 'non-natural qualities', others have spoken of an 'objective order of values', and others again have given a theistic interpretation to the objective correlate.[17] But, whatever the terminology, it is clear that the view is basically a Platonic one in its presupposition of the existence of values which cannot be reduced to any natural facts or combination of natural facts. Such a view, if it is philosophically intelligible, will certainly give us the required sort of objectivity. Can it give us practicality?

According to the non-naturalist a moral judgement involves the recognition of a moral truth which carries with it a tendency to action. In other words, a moral judgement will be said to involve both the making of an assertion (which may be true or false) and the expressing of a commitment to action; a cognitive and conative component are somehow linked together in the total activity of making a moral judgement. This type of view would escape some of the difficulties which can arise over the practicality of moral judgement if we construe moral belief as belief that a certain natural fact is the case. It amounts to saying that there is one special type of belief which is not inert, namely, the moral variety.

There are various difficulties in this view. The first is that it is not clear whether the basic notion—of cognition fused with conation—is intelligible. There seems to be a gap between believing that such and such is the case and being moved to act, in the sense that it is always possible to see the same facts and to adopt different attitudes. To argue thus, of course, is to do no more than reiterate the argument from the practicality of moral judgement which we discussed when it was used against naturalism. In that context we pointed out that it had no *general* validity, for certain definitions of value terms seem to retain the requisite practicality. In a similar way, a non-naturalist will argue that there is no reason why moral belief should resemble other kinds of belief in all respects; an upholder of a mixed cognition-conation theory could insist that moral belief is *sui generis*.

A second problem for a theory of this kind is that of freedom. It seems plausible to say that in general believing is passive rather than active. Beliefs are 'given'; we cannot choose whether to believe one thing rather than another. Now if moral belief is like this, and if it is thought to carry with it a full-blooded commitment to action, the agent's freedom of action is destroyed. It is just for this reason that Hare wishes to maintain that we can freely choose our ultimate moral views.[18] But this view would be rejected by a non-naturalist since it is incompatible with the objectivity he attributes to moral belief. He must therefore reject also a prescriptivist analysis of practicality. But this he can do. In the manner of the naturalist in the previous section he can say that moral cognition carries with it not necessarily commitment to action but some degree of motivation.

A third problem concerns the alleged autonomy of a person. In Chapter I we argued that persons are essentially self-determining and rule-following, and it may be pointed out that this is to say that they are autonomous. But, as we have just seen, an essential position of the non-naturalist is that persons cannot be autonomous in one sense: they are not free to choose their values, and they cannot make valid moral rules by their own self-legislation. This may at first sight suggest that the metaphysics of non-naturalism is inappropriate to respect-for-persons morality. The suggestion is misleading, however, since it arises from the confusion of several senses of the term 'autonomy'. Let us consider the most common of its senses in order to make it clear in which a non-naturalist can accept and in which he must reject the notion.

In the first place, to ascribe autonomy to a moral agent may be to say that his duty cannot be other than what he *thinks* he ought to do.[19] The non-naturalist can allow that a moral agent is autonomous in this sense, since it is consistent with holding that the agent may be mistaken. To ascribe autonomy in this sense does not mean, of course, that a man cannot be blamed for doing what he believes to be right. For there are times when we would blame a man for thinking in a certain manner. Secondly, to ascribe autonomy may be to say that a moral agent is essentially self-determining: he can and must choose *for himself* what he will do, for even if someone tells him what to do he has still to decide whether to obey the order. The non-naturalist will insist that a moral agent is autonomous in this sense, and it is the same sense which is implied in Chapter I when we say that persons are essentially self-determining and rule-following. But this second sense is frequently confused with a third, according to which a moral agent is said to be autonomous because he can himself create moral values, or make valid moral rules binding on all men simply in virtue of the legislative activity of the moral agent. This is the sense of 'autonomy' which the non-naturalist will deny, for he will maintain that the notions of 'creating a moral value' or 'making valid moral rules by self-legislation' are not really in the end intelligible. He can agree that moral agents formulate *conceptions* of values or that they formulate ideals, but he will maintain that such processes presuppose the logically prior notion of a value which is not created by the agent. If we put the point in terms of moral acts instead of values, the non-naturalist is distinguishing between 'choosing what to do' (which is 'autonomy' in the second sense) and 'choosing what we *ought* to do' (which is 'autonomy' in the third sense), and his claim is that the former is essential, and the latter impossible, for all moral agents.* It is clear, then, that the sense in which the non-naturalist denies autonomy is not the same as that which in Chapter I we found to be an essential feature of personality.

We assume, then, that the non-naturalist can meet the three difficulties which we have raised over his theory of practicality. How can we sum up his positive account? His position is that while we needs must be drawn to what we think to be right (the 'must' being a logical 'must' deriving from the conative nature of moral judgement) it is not the case that we needs must *choose* to do it. And this view, despite its difficulties, seems to fit the

---

* But notice that one can speak of *deciding* what one ought to do. This is because 'deciding' can have a cognitive sense; to decide what one ought to do is to decide *that* one ought to do A *rather than* B.

phenomenology of moral judgement. For it does seem both that we cannot choose what to think on these matters but can only report what we think we see, and that in the very seeing we are emotionally involved in some inevitable way. We are emotionally committed, one might say, but the involvement stops short of a decision to behave accordingly. Such a decision cannot be 'given' in the situation but must be freely taken by us. This, then, is the account of moral belief and its connexion with action which can be provided in terms of a non-naturalistic metaphysics of respect for persons.

The main difficulty with the non-naturalist position is simply that its assertion that there is an objective order of values (however it may be described) seems unverifiable and difficult to make sense of. The non-naturalist is arguing that moral judgements are the expressions of belief and that what makes the belief true is the existence of a realm of very dubious metaphysical status. How far can the non-naturalist meet objections to his metaphysics?

He can at least meet those which arise from the difficulties of intuitionism. Intuitionism is basically a doctrine of moral epistemology, but it has been thought to be a necessary counterpart to any doctrine of non-naturalism. Hence, the rejection of intuitionism has often been regarded as entailing the rejection of non-naturalism. But we wish to argue that non-naturalism does not necessarily involve intuitionism. Let us distinguish these positions.

First of all, it may be said that the non-naturalist is claiming that a moral judgement is true although he cannot support his belief by pointing to facts of an ordinary kind. It may therefore be maintained that his view commits him to saying with the intuitionist that we 'just see' that our moral judgements are true. The difficulty commonly raised over this position, however, is that it sounds as though the intuitionist is describing a familiar process we can all recognize, whereas few people are aware of any such characteristic process taking place when they make a moral judgement. But this objection need not be disturbing to the non-naturalist, for he is not committed to any view as to the process, or whatever, by which a moral judgement is made. His claim is simply that ordinary moral agents make moral judgements which they believe to be true, and he need not be disturbed if they also deny that they *see* anything with the moral eye or the eye of reason, or that any introspectible process goes on at all. Hence, while the intuitionist may be committed to some process of 'just seeing' the non-naturalist is not; the objection therefore does not touch his position.

Secondly, some forms of intuitionism are accused of stopping the search for justification at an arbitrary point. Now the theories which regard a bundle of unconnected principles as ultimate are perhaps open to this criticism. But since, as we have shown in Chapters I-III, it is possible to provide a single principle with reference to which others may be justified, a non-naturalist need not be criticized for stopping at an arbitrary point. It might, of course, be objected that in this chapter and elsewhere we speak not just of the respect-for-persons principle itself as true or false, but also of specific moral judgements. The reply is first that specific moral judgements are true or false in the sense of cohering or not with the wider principles of utility, equality, liberty, self-development etc., and ultimately with the respect-for-persons principle itself. But further, if they are true in this sense, they will also be true in the stronger objective sense. For the respect-for-persons principle can be said to be true in the strong sense, and whatever is entailed by a true proposition is itself true. Hence, non-naturalism can enable us to speak not only of the respect-for-persons principle but also of the specific moral judgements in which it is embodied as true or false without committing us to the difficulties of some forms of intuitionism.

Thirdly, a more serious criticism of intuitionism can be based on its claim to provide certain knowledge of a principle or judgement. The criticism can take more than one form. To begin with, it may be said that the intuitionist is committed to saying that he 'just knows' that he is right, but there is no way of arbitrating between his alleged insight and that of another intuitionist who likewise 'just knows' that a conflicting principle is right. Now this criticism is effective against intuitionism as a method of philosophical justification; for clearly a given principle is not justified by a method which would equally justify a conflicting principle. But the criticism need not be damaging to the non-naturalist if he makes no claims to demonstrating the truth of a moral principle but says only that moral judgement *presupposes* the existence of an objective order of values.

Another form of the same criticism rests on the premises that one cannot legitimately claim to know that something is the case if one

cannot produce convincing grounds to support the claim; and that
no grounds at all can be produced for an ultimate moral principle.
Now some philosophers might well dispute the first premise,
pointing out that mathematical, logical or other propositions (such
as that 'Nothing can be red and green all over') can be known to
be true without there being *grounds* for the claim to knowledge.
Fortunately, however, (whatever may be the predicament of the
intuitionist) the non-naturalist need not concern himself with this
controversy, for he need not maintain that the ordinary agent
knows that his moral judgements are true, but only that he firmly
believes that they are. And a claim to belief is not in the same way
dependent on convincing grounds as a claim to knowledge. Indeed,
the ordinary moral agent, although he cannot produce positive
grounds for his ultimate moral belief, can endeavour to win people
over to it by seeking confusions in the beliefs of others which may
render them untenable. For example, he may be able to show that
someone who believes in the importance of the community rather
than the individual is basing his belief on the mistaken notion of
the community as some entity over and above the individuals who
make it up. Again, he may be able to show that criticisms of his
own belief are based on a misunderstanding of it. In this indirect
and negative way the ordinary moral agent can show that there
is nothing irrational in holding his belief.

Fourthly, a slightly different sort of criticism of intuitionism
may be based on what we can call verificationism. It may be contended that there is no sense in talking of knowledge, or even of
belief, where the truth or falsity of one's belief can never be established, and where we cannot describe the nature of the facts which
render it true or false or the types of procedure which would lead
to verification or falsification. Can this familiar type of objection
to intuitionism be met in terms of the non-naturalist position?
To do so, we must distinguish between the various connected
claims which might be made by such an objector.

His claim that we cannot describe the facts asserted in moral
judgements except by reiterating the same remarks—a claim which
follows from the rejection of naturalism—need not worry us by
itself. There is no particular difficulty over verification in the case
of indefinable properties as such, since in general there is broad
agreement in actual predications among all word-users, and we can
specify the conditions under which the agreement will break down.

But it is not obvious what the corresponding method could be in the moral sphere. Thus it is not clear that we should count agreement among all moral agents as constituting verification of moral insights. Nor is there an obvious possibility of 'eschatological' verification. The Christian might maintain that ultimately we shall find out that the soul survives or that God exists. But in these cases we are talking of entities of which it might make sense to say that one would recognize them when one saw them, whereas in the moral case one has in mind a property which is supposed to belong to types of action. What kind of thing could one see in heaven which would bear out or contradict the belief that one type of action on earth was right and another wrong? There is therefore a strong case for saying that it is pointless to speak of moral beliefs (far less moral knowledge) if nothing can ever show them to be true or false.

To this argument the non-naturalist might reply that, if what we have said in this chapter is correct, moral agents have no option but to hold moral beliefs. The ordinary moral agent, we argued, sees morality as a matter of making *judgements* which can be true or false, and this practical conviction is ineradicable. Hence, an objective order of values is necessarily presupposed whether or not it is possible to provide an adequate theoretical account of it.

But someone who maintains that the absence of a verification procedure makes moral belief pointless may have a strong thesis in mind which would destroy the possibility of speaking of *holding* a view at all. For it might be said that we have been given no reason to assume that 'ought' has any meaning at all, or that people mean the same thing when they predicate it of actions. How can the meaning of a word be grasped, if there are no criteria for its correct use?

To this more radical thesis the non-naturalist can find a reply in terms of the characteristic guiding function of moral language. The child progresses from the stage of pure commands, accompanied by physical constraints or compulsions, to the stage where people say 'You ought' and back this up with reasons. He will see that these utterances are still often made for the purpose of getting him to do things. But he will also come to see that he is no longer being told to do something but rather told that something is the *case* in virtue of which he is expected to do something. For he will hear others discussing what one ought to do, as well as telling him what he ought to do. The non-naturalist need not be forced, then, into admitting that the moral 'ought' is meaningless, in the sense that consistency in its use cannot be secured. To establish the possibility of consistent usage of 'ought' is not, of course, to justify a particular statement in which it is used. Nevertheless, it does enable the non-naturalist to assert that the principle 'One ought to respect persons' or 'One ought to adopt the attitude of *agape*' expresses a belief which can be claimed as true. The difficulties in the intuitionist position are therefore not compelling when applied to the sort of non-naturalistic metaphysics which is fitting to the morality of respect for persons.

Despite this it may still be felt that the position of non-naturalism is unconvincing. Of course, to be unconvincing is not necessarily the same as to be incoherent or to fail to cover the facts. And it may be that if the view seems unconvincing it is simply because many Anglo-Saxon philosophers have a deep-rooted (and healthy) prejudice in favour of the empirical. There certainly does not seem to be any unanswerable objection to non-naturalism, and the phenomenology of moral experience—as that is seen from the standpoint of respect-for-persons morality—seems to make its presupposition at least plausible. Perhaps if we have expounded non-naturalism in a way which makes it at least plausible we have done as much as we can hope to do in an age of empiricism.

5 . CONCLUSION

In this chapter we have considered the meta-ethical or meta-physical views which might be appropriate to the morality of respect for persons as we have outlined it in Chapters I-III. A morality of respect for persons (and perhaps any morality whatso-ever) has certain logical features: it must be overriding, universal-izable, practical and objective. We rejected a meta-ethics of com-mitment as inappropriate to respect-for-persons morality since it excludes objectivity, relying merely on universalizability. The commitment theory has difficulty also in accommodating the phenomenon of moral perversity (although this difficulty is not connected specifically with respect-for-persons morality).

We considered next the metaphysics of naturalism. This type of view allows us to think of moral judgements as true or false, and one version—the 'good reasons' theory—can account for both objectivity and practicality in the relevant senses. It is unclear, however, whether this type of theory can make sense of the over-riding nature of a moral claim.

Finally, we considered the metaphysics of non-naturalism. We attempted to state this theory in as plausible a way as possible since it is by far the least fashionable of metaphysical theories of morality at the present. It can certainly give us objectivity in the strong sense we require, and it can combine this with practicality if a distinction is drawn between obligation and motivation. The stock objections to it—generally stated in the form of anti-intuitionist arguments—can be met. But in the end it leaves us with complex metaphysical commitments to the existence of an objective order of values.

We conclude, then, that if we are looking for a metaphysics appropriate to morality characterized in terms of the supreme regulative principle of respect for persons there are two possibilities, although neither is without difficulties: the naturalistic metaphysics of 'good reasons', and non-naturalism. In the language of a Consumers' Association investigation, they are the joint 'best buy', but neither can be recommended wholly without reservations.

APPENDIX

THE PRESUPPOSITION METHOD
OF JUSTIFICATION

In Chapters II and III we endeavoured to show that the principle of respect for persons is *presupposed* by the ordinary moral judgements commonly made in our society. This presupposition method is to be distinguished sharply from that used by R. S. Peters in his *Ethics and Education*, whereby he seeks to show that the practice of moral discourse, as part of the public language, loses its point if some kind of principle of respect for persons is not presupposed.* Peters thus derives the principle, not from the content of a particular set of moral judgements as we did in Chapters II and III, but from the form of moral discourse as such. And his hope is that by so doing he can provide a kind of justification for the respect-for-persons principle.

But even if we grant for the moment that participation in moral discourse involves the participants in observation of the respect-for-persons principle, we cannot show by this means that moral discoursers necessarily respect all human beings, but only that they must respect those with whom they practise moral discourse. For example, 'consideration of interests' is said to be built into participation in moral discourse on the grounds that sincere participation with others in a joint attempt to answer the question 'What ought I to do?' presupposes recognition of *their* claims to do what is in their interests. And this is a long way from respect for persons as such.

Peters would say here that all men, *qua* rational, must be regarded as possible contributors to the moral debate, since reason is the only criterion by which the value of a contribution to it may

* For a similar development of the presupposition method of argument see A. Phillips Griffiths, 'Ultimate Moral Principles: Their Justification' in *The Encyclopaedia of Philosophy*, edited by Paul Edwards, vol. 8, p. 178 ff. (New York, The Macmillan Co., 1967).

be judged. Now it is true that possession of reason is a necessary condition for anyone's contributing to any kind of debate. But a group of people discussing morality need not regard it as a sufficient condition. They can refuse to allow certain people to participate, without thereby disqualifying their discussion for the title of 'moral discourse', or causing it to lose its point. Moreover, they might back up their policy of exclusion with relevant reasons, and so forestall the possible objection that a rational activity (which the practice of moral discourse is assumed to be) must involve rational criteria of admittance to it. For example, they might limit their debating circle to those seen as having imagination, integrity and experience. If then respect for persons is the attitude people must have towards those with whom they discuss morality, it does not amount to respect for persons as such, but only to respect for the fellow-members of what they regard as the moral community.

But in any case it seems clear that respect for one's fellow-discoursers is not necessarily involved in the practice of moral discourse. It will be remembered that to respect a person is to make his ends one's own (show sympathy with him) and to take into account in one's dealings with him that he applies rules to himself and others. But imagine, for example, a soldier indoctrinated in some code of military honour engaging in moral discourse with a prisoner as to whether he ought to kill him or not. This would be a case of moral discourse but there would be no sympathy involved and hence no respect would be shown. It might be replied that, whereas the component of sympathy may not be presupposed in such a moral discourse, the situation does at least presuppose that the discoursers are willing to consider the applicability of each other's rules. But the soldier may not be interested in the prisoner's rules, but only in whether the prisoner thinks that this or that rule of military honour applies to the situation.

Peters might try to meet this example of the soldier by saying that it is not a case of the asking and answering of the question 'What ought I to do?' but rather a discourse on the question 'What does a certain code of behaviour prescribe for this occasion?' In other words, the discussion between the soldier and the prisoner is not a *basic* moral discussion, but proceeds on the assumption of certain moral hypotheses which are not themselves laid open to question. Having drawn this distinction, Peters might reformulate his thesis in terms of basic moral discourse, and say that it is the attempt to answer the question 'What ought I to do?' starting from scratch which presupposes respect for persons in the discoursers.

But this version of the thesis also collapses. For example, imagine a Greek asking an intelligent slave 'What ought I to do?' Here there could be moral discourse but no respect, for the owner would be regarding the slave as merely a 'tool with life'. It is certainly true that *rational* discourse of any kind (not just moral discourse) commits us to rejecting arbitrariness in favour of reasoned discussion, but it does not commit us to considering how far the specific moral rules of other men ought to be given sway in a certain situation. Far less does it commit us to making the ends of others our own. For example, the Greek slave-owner might with perfect consistency deny the slave any right to pursue his own interests, on the universalizable grounds that he is a slave. And if Peters wishes to say that a discourse in which this could happen is not a *moral* discourse, he is building too much specific content into his definition of 'moral discourse'—he is assuming from the start that discourse in which the participants do not respect each other is not moral discourse.

We therefore conclude that Peters cannot show that the respect for persons principle is presupposed in the practice of moral discourse; what can be shown is that the principle is presupposed by the content of a particular type of moral discourse. And this we have tried to do in Chapters II and III.

REFERENCES

CHAPTER I

1. P. Nowell-Smith, *Ethics*, p. 112 (London, Pelican Books, 1954).
2. R. M. Hare, *The Language of Morals*, p. 70 (Oxford University Press, 1952).
3. J. S. Mill, *On Liberty*, Chap. 3, p. 187 (London, Collins, The Fontana Library, edited by Mary Warnock, 1962).
4. For other objections to the 'rational will' analysis see W. G. Maclagan, 'Respect for Persons as a Moral Principle', Part 1, Section 3, *Philosophy*, July 1960.
5. Kant, *The Fundamental Principles of the Metaphysic of Morals*, translated by H. J. Paton as *The Moral Law*, pp. 90-91 (London, Hutchinson's University Library, 1948).
6. Kant, *op. cit.*, p. 98.
7. Maclagan, *op. cit.*, Section 8.
8. Maclagan, *op. cit.*, Section 8.
9. Bernard Williams, 'Morality and the Emotions', pp. 22-4, An Inaugural Lecture (London, 1965).
10. R. S. Downie, 'Forgiveness', *Philosophical Quarterly*, April 1964.
11. Bernard Williams, 'The Idea of Equality', pp. 114–20, in *Philosophy Politics and Society*, Second Series, edited by P. Laslett and W. G. Runciman (Oxford, Blackwell, 1964).
12. Dorothy Emmet, *Rules, Roles and Relations*, Chap. 8 (London, Macmillan, 1966).
13. The First Epistle of John, iv. 20.

CHAPTER II

1. J. S. Mill, *Utilitarianism*, Chap. 2, p. 257 (London, Collins, The Fontana Library, edited by Mary Warnock, 1962).
2. Mill, *op. cit.*, Chap. 2, p. 276.
3. For a discussion of Deontology, see D. Daiches Raphael, *Moral Judgement*, Chap. 3 (London, Allen and Unwin, 1955).
4. See J. Rawls, 'Two Concepts of Rules', *Philosophical Review*, 1955.

5. Mill, *op. cit.*, Chap. 5, pp. 318–20.

6. For a discussion of the concept of desert, see D. Daiches Raphael, *op. cit.*, pp. 67–79. Our whole discussion owes a great deal to the chapter on Justice in Raphael's book (pp. 62–94).

7. Aristotle, *Nicomachean Ethics*, Book V, Chap. 3.

8. Raphael, *op. cit.*, pp. 65–6.

9. Raphael, *op. cit.*, pp. 77–9.

10. See R. S. Peters, *Ethics and Education*, p. 128 (London, Allen and Unwin, 1966).

11. *Children and Their Primary Schools* (The Plowden Report) Chap. 5, esp. p. 57 (London, H.M.S.O., 1967).

12. Raphael, *op. cit.*, pp. 73–4.

13. R. M. Hare, *Freedom and Reason*, p. 178 (Oxford University Press, 1963).

14. J. S. Mill, *On Liberty*, Chap. 1, p. 135 (London, Collins, The Fontana Library, edited by Mary Warnock, 1962).

15. For a discussion of this question, see W. G. Maclagan, 'How Important Is Moral Goodness?', *Mind* 1955.

16. For a discussion of the concept of fraternity, see R. S. Peters, *op. cit.*, pp. 215–27.

17. R. S. Peters, *op. cit.*, p. 216. Compare also the passage quoted earlier (p. 54) on justice and utility from Raphael, *op. cit.*

CHAPTER III

1. The following discussion of private morality is largely based on a paper by R. S. Downie delivered to the Aristotelian Society in February 1968, and published in the *Proceedings of the Aristotelian Society* for 1967–68. We are indebted to the Society for permission to make use of the material.

2. David P. Gauthier, *Practical Reasoning*, p. 147 (Oxford University Press, 1963).

3. D. Daiches Raphael, *Moral Judgement*, p. 117, *passim* (London, Allen and Unwin, 1955).

4. P. Nowell-Smith, *Ethics*, pp. 198, 211, 310, 210–11, 228–9 (London, Pelican Books, 1954).

5. P. F. Strawson, 'Social Morality and Individual Ideal', *Philosophy*, 1961.

6. J. S. Mill, *On Liberty*, Chap. 1, p. 135 (London, Collins, The Fontana Library, edited by Mary Warnock, 1962).

7. For discussions of prudence, see W. G. Maclagan, 'Self and Others: A Defence of Altruism', *Philosophical Quarterly*, April 1954; J. D. Mabbott and H. J. N. Horsburgh, 'Prudence', *The Aristotelian Society, Sup. Vol.* XXXVI, 1962; R. S. Peters and A. P. Griffiths, 'The Autonomy of Prudence', *Mind*, 1962; W. D. Falk, 'Morality, Self and Others' in *Morality and the Language of Conduct*, edited by H.-N. Castañeda and G. Nakhnikian (Detroit, Wayne State University Press, 1963).

8. For a discussion of the consistency of the doctrines of *Utilitarianism* with those of *On Liberty*, see R. S. Downie, 'Mill on Pleasure and Self-Development', *Philosophical Quarterly*, January 1966.

9. Mill, *op. cit.*, Chap. 3, p. 188.

10. Mill, *op. cit.*, Chap. 3, p. 187.

11. Mill, *op. cit.*, Chap. 3, p. 188.

12. Cf. C. A. Campbell, 'Are There "Degrees" of the Moral Emotion?', *Mind*, 1936, reprinted in *In Defence of Free-Will* (London, Allen and Unwin, 1967).

13. J. O. Urmson, 'Saints and Heroes', in *Essays in Moral Philosophy*, edited by A. I. Melden (Seattle, University of Washington Press, 1958).

14. Bernard Mayo, 'Human Rights', pp. 226–31, *The Aristotelian Society Sup. Vol.* XXXIX, 1965, reprinted in *Political Theory and the Rights of Man*, edited by D. D. Raphael (London, Macmillan, 1967).

15. Cf. W. G. Maclagan, *op. cit.*

16. Cf. E. F. Carritt, 'An Ambiguity of the Word "Good",' *Proceedings of the British Academy*, 1937.

17. The discussion of self-respect is based on a paper by Elizabeth Telfer in *Philosophical Quarterly*, April 1968. We are indebted to the Editor for permission to use some of the material.

18. Aristotle, *Nicomachean Ethics*, Book IX, Chap. 8.

CHAPTER IV

1. There are, of course, empiricists who do not subscribe to the regularity theory of causation. See, for example, R. J. Hirst, *The Problems of Perception*, pp. 98–9 (London, Allen and Unwin, 1959).

2. W. D. Ross, *Foundations of Ethics*, Chap. 10 (Oxford University Press, 1939).

3. For a discussion of the relationships between desires, causes and action, see A. Kenny, *Action, Emotion and Will*, Chap. V (London, Routledge and Kegan Paul, 1963).

4. G. Ryle, *The Concept of Mind*, Chap. 4 (London, Hutchinson's University Library, 1949).

5. See B. F. McGuinness, 'I Know What I Want', *Proc. Arist. Soc.* 1957.

6. S. Hampshire, in D. F. Pears (editor), *Freedom and the Will*, Chap. 6 (London, Macmillan, 1963).

7. C. D. Broad, 'Determinism, Indeterminism and Libertarianism', in *Ethics and the History of Philosophy*, esp. p. 204 (London, Routledge and Kegan Paul, 1952).

8. P. F. Strawson, in Pears, *op. cit.*, Chap. 4.

9. P. F. Strawson, 'Freedom and Resentment', *Proceedings of the British Academy*, vol. XLVIII, 1962. Our criticisms of Strawson are based on R. S. Downie, 'Objective and Reactive Attitudes', *Analysis*, 27.2, December 1966. We are indebted to the editor of *Analysis* for permission to use some of the material from this article.

10. Strawson, *op. cit.*, pp. 194-5.

11. Strawson, *op. cit.*, p. 197.

12. Strawson, *op. cit.*, p. 195.

13. Richard Taylor, *Action and Purpose*, Chaps. 10, 14 (New Jersey, Prentice Hall, 1966). Taylor provides an interesting critique of the empiricist analysis of causation, and in general puts forward a view of action with which we have much sympathy.

14. P. F. Strawson, *Introduction to Logical Theory*, Chap. 9 (London, Methuen, 1952).

CHAPTER V

1. For a discussion which takes a rather different line from our own on the question of the content of morality, see G. J. Warnock, *Contemporary Moral Philosophy*, pp. 55-61 (London, Macmillan, New Studies in Ethics, 1967).

2. But see C. H. Whiteley, 'On Defining "Moral",' *Analysis*, 1959-60, for the opposite view.

3. R. S. Peters, *Ethics and Education*, p. 121 (London, Allen and Unwin, 1966).

4. See Alasdair MacIntyre, *A Short History of Ethics*, *passim*, especially Chapter 18 (London, Routledge and Kegan Paul, 1967).

5. R. M. Hare, *Freedom and Reason*, p. 5 *et passim* (Oxford University Press, 1963).

6. Hare, *op. cit.*, p. 106 *et passim*.

7. J.-P. Sartre, *Existentialism and Humanism*, (London, Methuen, 1966).

8. Peters, *op. cit.*, p. 99.

9. Aristotle, *Nichomachean Ethics*, Book VII, Chapter 3.

10. G. E. Moore, *Principia Ethica*, Chapter I (Cambridge University Press, 1903, 1959 (paperback edition)).

11. G. E. Moore, *op. cit.*, p. 15.

12. R. M. Hare, *The Language of Morals*, Chapter V (Oxford University Press, 1952).

13. An important exponent of this view is Mrs P. Foot. See her 'Moral Beliefs', *Proceedings of the Aristotelian Society*, 1958-9; 'Moral Arguments', *Mind*, 1958; 'Goodness and Choice', *Aristotelian Society Sup. Vol.*, 1961.

14. Butler, *Sermon III*, Sects. 8-9 (edited by W. R. Matthews, London, Bell and Sons, 1964).

15. Plato, *Republic*, 352b *et passim*.

16. P. Foot, 'Moral Beliefs', p. 104, *Proceedings of the Aristotelian Society*, 1958-59.

17. For a rigorous discussion of this elusive subject see W. G. Maclagan, *The Theological Frontier of Ethics*, especially Chapter III, Sections 15-20 and Appendix Note B (London, Allen and Unwin, 1961).

18. R. M. Hare, *Freedom and Reason*, p. 2 (Oxford University Press, 1963).

19. For a discussion of the grounds of duty see W. G. Maclagan, 'On Being Sure of One's Duty', *Philosophical Quarterly*, October 1950.

INDEX

GEORGE ALLEN & UNWIN LTD

Head Office
40 Museum Street, London, W.C.1
Telephone: 01-405 8577

Sales, Distribution and Accounts Departments
Park Lane, Hemel Hempstead, Herts.
Telephone: 0442 | 3244

Athens: 34 Panepistimiou Street
Auckland: P.O. Box 36013, Northcote Central N.4
Barbados: P.O. Box 222, Bridgetown
Bombay: 103/5 Fort Street, Bombay 1
Buenos Aires: Escritorio 454-459, Florida 165
Beirut: Deeb Building, Jeanne d'Arc Street
Calcutta: 285J Bepin Behari Ganguli Street, Calcutta 12
Cape Town: 68 Shortmarket Street
Hong Kong: 105 Wing On Mansion, 26 Hancow Road, Kowloon
Ibadan: P.O. Box 62
Karachi: Karachi Chambers, McLeod Road
Madras: 2/18 Mount Road, Madras
Mexico: Villalongin 32, Mexico 5, D.F.
Nairobi: P.O. Box 30583
New Delhi: 13-14 Asaf Ali Road, New Delhi 1
Philippines: P.O. Box 157, Quezon City D-502
Rio de Janeiro: Caixa Postal 2537-Zc-00
Singapore: 36c Prinsep Street, Singapore 7
Sydney N.S.W.: Bradbury House, 55 York Street
Tokyo: C.P.O. Box 1728, Tokyo 100-91
Toronto: 81 Curlew Drive, Don Mills

CONSTANTIN BRUNNER
SCIENCE, SPIRIT, SUPERSTITION

THE BASIC PRINCIPLES OF HUMAN THOUGHT

This book is a synopsis of the work of an original thinker, whom Albert Schweitzer called 'a congenial mind'. Brunner's theory of the three faculties of thought (Fakultätenlehre) gives us an all-embracing view of man's outer and inner world. Perhaps the greatest merit of Brunner as a philosopher is that he has added to our materialistic and idealistic faculties of thought the third faculty of fictitious thinking or the *Analogon*. Analogous or superstitious thought is a perverted imitation of genuine spiritual creativity. Man, in his unrestrained egoism, affixes material qualities to the inspired thought of essential being in its infinity and eternity, and superstition is thus seen to be a mental disease of mankind hitherto undiagnosed, and the cause of many sufferings.

The concept of the three faculties of thought proves itself a valuable critical guide to the deeper understanding of all human endeavour and accomplishment. The scientist will find here the ideas so vitally needed to complement his speciality, and further he will discover a fascinating history of cross-fertilization between science and philosophy. The artist will gain insight into his enigmatic world of imagination and creativity, and students of theology will discover unusually clear frescoes of mystic thought that provide new dimensions to the personality of Christ. Although written in the grand tradition of philosophical systems, this book often addresses the reader directly, and by so doing activates his thinking.

Students of all disciplines will find this book fascinating, and their search for an anchorage of scientific thought on deeper spiritual ground will not fail to be satisfied.

'Students from a wide field will find this book an excellent medium for a closer understanding of human aims and accomplishments.' *Liverpool Daily Post*

'In an age which lives upon little thoughts, the grandeur and open horizon of Brunner's teachings shine with a strange radiance giving light and not heat.' *Jewish Quarterly*

LONDON: GEORGE ALLEN AND UNWIN LTD

S